THE
MICHELIN
GUIDE

CHICAGO
2018

THE MICHELIN GUIDE'S COMMITMENTS

Whether they are in Japan, the USA, China or Europe, our inspectors apply the same criteria to judge the quality of each and every establishment that they visit. The MICHELIN guide commands a **worldwide reputation** thanks to the commitments we make to our readers—and we reiterate these below:

Our inspectors make **anonymous visits** to restaurants to gauge the quality of cuisine offered to the everyday customer. They pay their own bill and make no indication of their presence. These visits are supplemented by comprehensive monitoring of information—our readers' comments are one valuable source, and are always taken into consideration.

Our choice of establishments is a completely **independent** one, made for the benefit of our readers alone. Decisions are discussed by inspectors and editor, with the most important considered at the global level. Inclusion in the Guide is always free of charge.

The Guide offers a **selection** of the best restaurants in each category of comfort and price. A recommendation in the Guide is an honor in itself, and defines the establishment among the "best of the best."

All practical information, the classifications, and awards are revised and updated every year to ensure the most **reliable information** possible.

The standards and criteria for the classifications are the same in all countries covered by the MICHELIN guides. Our system is used worldwide and easy to apply when selecting a restaurant.

As part of Michelin's ongoing commitment to improving **travel and mobility**, we do everything possible to make vacations and eating out a pleasure.

THE MICHELIN GUIDE'S SYMBOLS

AVERAGE PRICES

💰	Under $25
$$	$25 to $50
$$$	$50 to $75
$$$$	Over $75

FACILITIES & SERVICES

	Notable wine list
	Notable cocktail list
	Notable beer list
	Notable sake list
	Wheelchair accessible
	Outdoor dining
	Private dining room
	Breakfast
	Brunch
	Dim sum
BYO	Bring your own
	Valet parking
	Cash only

RESTAURANT CLASSIFICATIONS BY COMFORT
More pleasant if in red

	Small plates
	Comfortable
	Quite comfortable
	Very comfortable
	Top class comfortable
	Luxury in the traditional style

STARS

Our famous one ✿, two ✿✿ and three ✿✿✿ stars
identify establishments serving the highest quality
cuisine – taking into account the quality of ingredients,
the mastery of techniques and flavors, the levels of
creativity and, of course, consistency.

✿✿✿ Exceptional cuisine, worth a special journey
✿✿ Excellent cuisine, worth a detour
✿ High quality cooking, worth a stop

BIB GOURMAND

Inspectors' favorites for good value.

MICHELIN PLATE

Good cooking.
Fresh ingredients, carefully
prepared: simply a good meal.

DEAR READER,

It's been an exciting year for the entire team at the MICHELIN guides in North America, and it is with great pride that we present you with our 2018 edition to Chicago. Over the past year our inspectors have extended their reach to include a variety of establishments and multiplied their anonymous visits to restaurants in our selection in order to accurately reflect the rich culinary diversity this great city has to offer.

As part of the Guide's highly confidential and meticulous evaluation process, our inspectors have methodically eaten their way through the entire city with a mission to marshal the finest in each category for your enjoyment. While they are expertly trained professionals in the food industry, the Guides remain consumer-driven and provide comprehensive choices to accommodate your every comfort, taste, and budget. By dining and drinking as "everyday" customers, they are able to experience and evaluate the same level of service and cuisine as any other guest. This past year has seen some unique advancements in Chicago's dining scene. Some of these can be found in each neighborhood introduction, complete with photography depicting our favored choices.

Our company's founders, Édouard and André Michelin, published the first MICHELIN guide in 1900, to provide motorists with useful information about where they could service and repair their cars as well as find a good quality meal. In 1926, the star-rating system was introduced, whereby outstanding establishments are awarded for excellence in cuisine. Over the decades we have made many new enhancements to the Guide, and the local team here in Chicago eagerly carries on these traditions.

As we take consumer feedback seriously, please feel free to contact us at: michelin.guides@michelin.com. You may also follow our Inspectors on Twitter (@MichelinGuideCH) and Instagram (@michelininspectors) as they chow their way around town. We thank you for your patronage and truly hope that the MICHELIN guide will remain your preferred reference to Chicago's restaurants.

CONTENTS

CHICAGO

ANDERSONVILLE, EDGEWATER & UPTOWN

LINCOLN SQUARE · RAVENSWOOD

A walk through Chicago's North side, rich with culinary traditions from centuries of immigrant settlers, is like globe-trotting. A number of local businesses, specialty stores, row houses, and hotels populate the quaint streets of Andersonville, and architecture buffs never grow weary of the numerous art deco buildings set along Bryn Mawr Avenue and Lake Michigan's beaches.

HOW SWEDE IT IS

A water tower emblazoned with the blue-and-yellow Swedish flag rises above Clark Street, proudly representing Andersonville's Nordic roots. Step inside the Swedish-American Museum for a history lesson. Then head to one of the last Swedish emporiums in the area— **Wikstrom's Specialty Foods'** online-only gift shop—to take home a bag of red fish or even meatballs and herring among other packaged goods. Most early birds can be found lining up for coffee and creative breakfast plates (sassy eggs or frazzled eggs, anyone?) at **Over Easy Café**, while heartier appetites won't be able to resist the Viking breakfast at **Svea Restaurant** featuring piles of Swedish-style pancakes, sausages, and toasted limpa bread.

Beyond the well-represented Scandinavian community, Andersonville also brings the world to its doorstep thanks to those amply stocked shelves at **Middle East Bakery & Grocery**. Their deli selection includes a spectrum of spreads, breads, olives, and hummus, thereby making it entirely feasible to throw a meze feast in a matter of minutes. However, if your tastes run further south (of the border), then **Isabella Bakery** is a gem for all things Guatemalan—and turns out a host of tamales to die for. Adventurous foodies depend on the grocery section to keep their pantries stocked with fresh spices, dried fruits, rosewater, nuts, teas, and more.

AN ASIAN AFFAIR

Across town, the pagoda-style roof of the Argyle El stop on the Red Line serves as another visual clue to the plethora of eats available here. Imagine an East Asian lineup of Chinese, Thai, and Vietnamese restaurants, noodle shops, delis, bakeries, and herbalists. Platters of lacquered, bronzed duck and pork make **Sun Wah BBQ** an inviting and popular spot for Cantonese cuisine, while **dak Korean** is a perpetual cult favorite for spicy chicken wings and rice bowls served from a counter. And for those less inclined to cook for themselves, a genesis of casual eateries is prospering along these streets. **BopNgrill,** for instance, specializes in Asian fusion food like *loco moco*, as well as

and deli items at **Gene's Sausage Shop**. For a more refined selection of chops, steaks and free-range poultry, head to **Lincoln Quality Meat Market**. And speaking of meat treats, **Wolfy's** serves one of the best red-hots in Uptown, piling its dogs with piccalilli, pickles, peppers, and other rainbow-colored condiments. Its iconic neon sign (a crimson frankfurter jauntily pierced by a pitchfork) only intensifies the urge to stop here.

signatures like the fantastically messy kimchi burger, featuring caramelized kimchi, fried egg, sharp cheddar, bacon, and spicy mayo. Finally, make sure to stop by **Little Vietnam** on Bryn Mawr for affordable salads, sandwiches, and that divine bowl of steaming *pho*.

MEAT, POTATOES —AND MORE

Chicagoans can't resist a good sausage, so find them giving thanks regularly to the German immigrants who helped develop Lincoln Square and whose appreciation for fine meats still resonates in this neighborhood. Old World-inspired butchers ply their trade, stuffing wursts and offering specialty meats

For dinner party essentials, (think vegetables, fruits, flowers and more), Andersonville boasts a farmer's market in most areas and most days of the week. However, the **Andersonville Farmer's Market** in particular (held on Wednesdays) is home to an impressive number of bakeries, as well as an orchard's worth of Asian fruit. Then of course there's the **Lincoln Square Farmer's Market**, which throws its doors open like clockwork on Tuesdays, and hosts live music during market hours every Thursday evening. And also settled in Lincoln Square is **HarvesTime Foods**, a culinary bazaar that wears its sustainability on its sleeve. Imagine a solar-paneled roof set above a massive lineup of regionally sourced produce and you know that you've arrived at the right spot.

Along the same lines, Edgewater's **Sauce and Bread Kitchen** (which is a collaboration between beloved artisans **Co-op Sauce** and **Crumb Chicago**) brings two of the Windy City's favorite local products together at one location (read: café). Made-to-order breakfast and lunch sandwiches filled with maple sausage or applewood-smoked turkey are lavished with house-made condiments like tomato sauce (a fan favorite and fittingly so), while other party treats like hot sauce have a near-cultish following.

RAISE A GLASS

Critically acclaimed as one of the country's best boutique coffee shops, **The Coffee Studio** pours a mean cup of joe. Their locally roasted brews pair perfectly with a box of the "glazed & infused" doughnuts, which may need to be ordered in advance. In Edgewater, the creative community convenes at **The Metropolis Café**, an offshoot of Chicago's own **Metropolis Coffee Company**. Searching for something stronger than caffeine to bring to your next reservation? As the name suggests, family-owned producers and small-batch offerings are the focus at **Independent Spirits Inc.**, a wine and liquor shop replete with global selections.

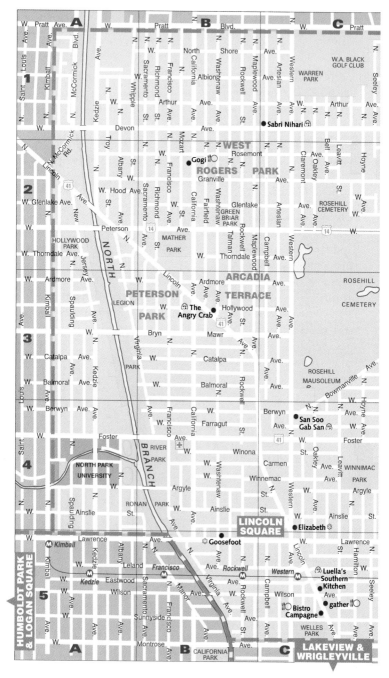

A

W. Pratt Ave.
W. Pratt
Blvd.
Pratt
W.

North Shore Ave.

California
Washtenaw
Maplewood Ave.
Artesian Ave.
Western Ave.

W.A. BLACK GOLF CLUB

WARREN PARK

Albion

1

Devon Ave.

● Sabri Nihari 🍴

Arthur Ave.

Seeley

Bell Ave.
Leavitt Ave.
Hoyne

Claremont Ave.
Oakley Ave.

WEST ROGERS PARK

Rosemont

● Gogi 🍴

Granville

Glenlake

ROSEHILL CEMETERY

GREEN BRIAR PARK

2

W. Glenlake Ave.

W. Hood Ave.

Peterson

MATHER PARK

Thorndale

Rosehill

Artesian Ave.

Western Ave.

HOLLYWOOD PARK

W. Thorndale Ave.

Lincoln

ARCADIA TERRACE

Ardmore Ave.

ROSEHILL CEMETERY

Ardmore Ave.

NORTH

PETERSON PARK

LEGION

🦀 The Angry Crab ●

Hollywood Ave.

3

Catalpa Ave.

Bryn

Mawr

Catalpa

ROSEHILL MAUSOLEUM

Balmoral Ave.

Balmoral

Bowmanville

Berwyn Ave.

Berwyn Ave.

● San Soo Gab San 🍴

Hoyne

4

Foster

RIVER PARK

Farragut

Winona

Foster

Oakley Ave.
Leavitt Ave.

WINNEMAC PARK

NORTH PARK UNIVERSITY

Carmen

Winnemac

Argyle

Argyle

Ainslie

Ainslie

RONAN PARK

LINCOLN SQUARE

● Elizabeth ✿

Lawrence

🅜 Kimball

Leland

Lawrence

✿ Goosefoot

Hamilton

Seeley

🅜 Kedzie
Eastwood

Francisco

Western 🅜

🍴 Luella's Southern Kitchen

5

Wilson

Wilson

gather 🍴

🍴 Bistro Campagne

Sunnyside

WELLES PARK

HUMBOLDT PARK & LOGAN SQUARE

Montrose

CALIFORNIA PARK

LAKEVIEW & WRIGLEYVILLE

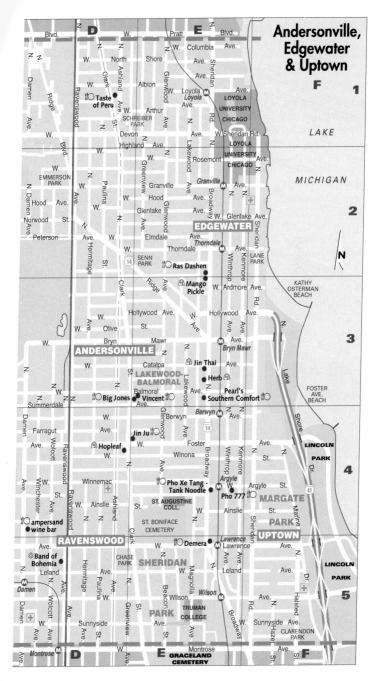

Andersonville, Edgewater & Uptown

Pratt Blvd.
Columbia Ave.
North Shore Ave.
Albion Ave.
Loyola Ave.
LOYOLA UNIVERSITY CHICAGO
Arthur Ave.
SCHREIBER PARK
Devon Ave.
Highland Ave.
W. Sheridan Rd.
LOYOLA UNIVERSITY CHICAGO
Rosemont Ave.

Taste of Peru

LAKE MICHIGAN

Granville Ave.
Granville Ave.
Hood Ave.
Glenlake Ave.
Glenlake Ave.
Elmdale Ave.
Thorndale Ave.
Thorndale Ave.

EMMERSON PARK
Hood Ave.
Norwood Ave.
Peterson Ave.

EDGEWATER

SENN PARK

Ras Dashen

Mango Pickle

LANE PARK
KATHY OSTERMAN BEACH

Ardmore Ave.
Hollywood Ave.
Hollywood Ave.
Olive Ave.
Bryn Mawr
Bryn Mawr Ave.

ANDERSONVILLE

Catalpa Ave.
Jin Thai
LAKEWOOD-BALMORAL
Herb
Balmoral Ave.
Pearl's Southern Comfort
Big Jones
Vincent
Summerdale Ave.

FOSTER AVE. BEACH

Berwyn Ave.
Farragut Ave.
Berwyn
Jin Ju
Foster Ave.
Hopleaf
Winona Ave.
Winnemac Ave.
Pho Xe Tang - Tank Noodle
Pho 777
Argyle St.
Argyle St.
Ainslie St.
ST. AUGUSTINE COLL.
Ainslie St.
ST. BONIFACE CEMETERY

LINCOLN PARK

MARGATE PARK

UPTOWN

ampersand wine bar

RAVENSWOOD
CHASE PARK
Demera
Lawrence Ave.
Lawrence Ave.

Band of Bohemia
Leland Ave.
Leland Ave.

LINCOLN PARK

SHERIDAN PARK
Wilson Ave.
Wilson Ave.
Beacon
TRUMAN COLLEGE

Damen
Sunnyside Ave.
Sunnyside Ave.
CLARENDON PARK

Montrose Ave.
Montrose Ave.
GRACELAND CEMETERY

N

AMPERSAND WINE BAR 🍴

American

XX | 🍸 ♿

MAP: D4

This cool wine bar cuts a stylish figure with its pale walls, gorgeous blonde wood, and sun-flooded dining room. Combine that urbane setting with polished service and a simple, but perfectly executed menu and you have one consistently great Chicago spot. Grab a seat at the long, L-shaped bar, the best perch in the house to ask a zillion questions—or just dig in as the small plates begin their march from behind the counter.

The menu may be small, but it still packs a big punch—what's available is seasonal, diverse, and extremely fresh. A cold and creamy gold tomato gazpacho features tart strips of roasted eggplant and cool cucumber; while a deconstructed strawberry shortcake arrives in layers of luscious basil caramel and sweet berries.

■ 4845 N. Damen Ave. (bet. Ainslie St. & Lawrence Ave.)
🚇 Damen (Brown)
📞 (773) 728-0031 — **WEB:** www.ampersandchicago.com
■ Dinner Tue – Sun

PRICE: $$

THE ANGRY CRAB 😊

Seafood

🍴 | ♿ BYO

MAP: B3

Don't be shellfish—bring friends, beer, and wine to dinner at The Angry Crab for a messy, more-the-merrier experience. Lines form nightly for the chance to fill up on a Cajun-style spread shot through with Vietnamese flavors that reflect the owners' heritage.

Order from the laminated menus or the large overhead chalkboard for a seafood feast with options like whole head-on shrimp or enormous snow crab legs. Pick from a choice of lemon, garlic, or spicy sauces, stake your claim on a roll of paper towels and a seat at the communal tables, and then rip open the plastic bags in which the seafood arrives and dig in with your claws. Still hungry? Make it a true crab boil and add sausage, corn on the cob, and red bliss potatoes to round out the meal.

■ 5665 N. Lincoln Ave. (bet. Fairfield & Washtenaw Aves.)
📞 (773) 784-6848 — **WEB:** www.theangrycrabchicago.com
■ Lunch Sat – Sun   Dinner nightly

PRICE: $$

BAND OF BOHEMIA ✾
Gastropub

XX | 🍸 🍺 🍴 & 🖾

MAP: D5

So much more than a working brewery with a talented kitchen, Band of Bohemia is in fact a truly inspired gastropub that produces its own utterly unique creations both in the glass and on the plate.

Located in a repurposed brick building across from the Metra tracks, the look is understandably industrial, with an open layout that unwinds into a series of seating options, inviting bar, and an open kitchen with another small bar set against pretty blue tiles. Curved, high-backed booths lend intimacy to counter the room's sheer size. Stainless steel tanks displayed in the back hold the culinary-minded handiwork of their head brewer. On tap, expect a handful of rotating beers like the Coconut ESB, a copper-hued ale brewed with toasted fennel, coriander seeds, and coconut sugar.

Those rich brews are matched seamlessly to the kitchen's boundless small and large plates, which defy expectations with delicious success. Change is a virtue of the menu, but hits have included fresh pasta tinted green from nettles and tossed with aged goat cheese, toasted hazelnuts, and charred allium. The banana curry is a wonder of spicy and sweet notes from roasted cauliflower, smoky eggplant, goat's milk caramel, and peanuts.

▨ 4710 N. Ravenswood Ave. (bet. Lawrence & Leland Aves.)
🚇 Damen (Brown)
✆ (773) 271-4710 — **WEB:** www.bandofbohemia.com
▨ Lunch Sat – Sun Dinner Tue – Sun   **PRICE:** $$

19

BIG JONES ⅇ○
Southern

✗✗ | 🍸 🛋 ⚖

At Big Jones, guests are greeted with a "Guide to Good Drinking": a menu that includes barrel-aged punch selections and an impressive lineup of Bourbon and whiskey. Between that, the high bar tables, and plush velvet touches, this is a guaranteed good time. Yes, it's no front porch in Louisiana, but it's certainly close.

The menu is filled with dishes that reach back in Southern history and the service staff loves to dive into ancient detail. But this does not mean that the delicious cuisine doesn't explain itself: one may look forward to the likes of homemade pimento cheese with out-of-this-world Tasso ham cured in-house; or spot-on crawfish étouffee swimming with butter and wine and served atop a fluffy mound of spicy, smoky Braggadocio rice.

■ 5347 N. Clark St. (bet. Balmoral & Summerdale Aves.)
■ Berwyn
✆ (773) 275-5725 — **WEB:** www.bigjoneschicago.com
■ Lunch & dinner daily   PRICE: $$

BISTRO CAMPAGNE ⅇ○
French

✗✗ | 🛋 ⊡ ⚖

The romantic ideal of a French bistro is alive and well at quaint Bistro Campagne, where a tiny bar by the entrance is ready with your aperitif. Light slants through wooden Venetian blinds, bouncing off cream-and-brick walls in the welcoming dining room. Choose a white cloth-covered table inside or go outside under the garden's twinkling lights and green tree branches.

Inspired accompaniments make for memorable versions of rustic French standards. Start with a large, savory bowl of soupe à l'oignon gratinée capped with a thick layer of melting Gruyère. Then, discover their pitch-perfect duck pithiviers, wild mushroom duxelles and hazelnuts in puff pastry with a Madeira reduction. Brown butter pain perdu tucked with black figs is moist and delicious.

■ 4518 N. Lincoln Ave. (bet. Sunnyside & Wilson Aves.)
■ Western (Brown)
✆ (773) 271-6100 — **WEB:** www.bistrocampagne.com
■ Lunch Sun Dinner nightly   PRICE: $$

DEMERA ⚍

Ethiopian

✗ | ♿   **MAP:** E5

Demera's well-lit corner location welcomes hungry Uptown residents looking to immerse themselves in Ethiopian cuisine. Colorful wicker seating at the dining room's communal table gives groups an authentic dining experience, while picture windows offer plenty of people-watching for everyone.

Vegetarian and omnivorous offerings abound on the menu, which features a small glossary of terms to help newcomers. Pleasantly spicy yesiga wot combines tender chunks of beef with onions and ginger in a rich berbere sauce. Served with turmeric-infused split peas and jalapeño-laced collard greens, this stew is a hearty pleasure. Sop up extra sauce with piles of tangy and soft injera, presented in the traditional Ethiopian manner in lieu of silverware.

▇   4801 N. Broadway (at Lawrence Ave.)
▇   Lawrence
✆   (773) 334-8787 — **WEB:** www.demeraethiopian.com
▇   Lunch & dinner daily   **PRICE:** $$

GATHER ⚍

American

✗✗ | ♿ 🎪 📷 🥡   **MAP:** C5

A chic, cozy space lets guests get up close and personal at gather. Diners seeking dinner and a show take front row seats at barstools lining the open kitchen's polished granite counter, while tall communal tables fill with patrons enjoying bites from the menu's "gather and share" section. A rear dining room offers more solitude and romance.

Family-style Sunday dinners are a local draw, but the à la carte menu showcases flavorful options nightly. Slice into a single large uovo raviolo to mingle poached egg and ricotta with white truffle butter, jalapeño slivers, and chopped chives, or share a crock of Pernod-splashed mussels. Fragrant and garlicky, they're served with sourdough toast points for soaking up every last drop of the white wine-cream sauce.

▇   4539 N. Lincoln Ave. (bet. Sunnyside & Wilson Aves.)
▇   Western (Brown)
✆   (773) 506-9300 — **WEB:** www.gatherchicago.com
▇   Lunch Sat – Sun   Dinner nightly   **PRICE:** $$

ELIZABETH ✿
Contemporary

✕✕

Elizabeth is a restaurant that endeavors to tell a story—one that explores land and sea through contemporary American cuisine.

The diminutive interior has only a handful of tables, each with views of the brightly lit kitchen. The whitewashed tin ceiling and shelves stocked with everything from Dutch ovens to jars of pickles make it seem like we're all dining in Chef Iliana Regan's cottage-chic underground restaurant. You might even see her refilling your water glass; this is a passionate place where dedication trumps attitude.

The nightly multi-course menu is a clear treatise on local, organic and foraged cuisine. Don't be surprised to be served a gnarled log, laden with wild mushrooms and grains stuffed into cabbage leaves, or a quail's nest containing rye, fromage blanc, and topped with a soft-cooked egg. House breads can be an extraordinary highlight, including sourdough with tallow-enriched butter and walnut bitters, as well as nori bread served with bonito-infused butter and topped with caviar. Desserts may be inspired by the sea, as in the glass terrarium of pistachio sponge cake, dots of birch-flavored ice cream, blueberry sorbet, foraged herbs, and seashell-shaped kefir gummies.

4835 N. Western, Unit D (bet. Ainslie St. & Lawrence Ave.)
Western (Brown)
☎ (773) 681-0651 — **WEB:** www.elizabeth-restaurant.com
Dinner Tue – Sat

PRICE: $$$$

GOGI ⑪O

Korean

✗✗   **MAP:** B2

The surging popularity of Korean food continues to flourish along these shores of Lake Michigan. And as foodies would have you know, Gogi is one of the best places in the city to experience it. With its hip, industrial décor, imposing exhaust fans over each table (a clear sign that there's a ton of grilling going on), and lively blend of sweet, spicy, and sour flavors, dinner here promises to be a sensory explosion like no other.

One could feast on the abundant pre-meal banchan alone—a stunning selection of kimchi, mirin-soaked fish cakes, sake-steamed black beans, and more. But, that would mean missing out on delicate slices of sirloin bulgogi smothered in a sweet, gingery marinade; or restorative, spicy sundubu jjigae bubbling away in an iron pot.

▧ 6240 N.California Ave. (bet. Granville & Rosemont Aves.)
℘ (773) 274-6669 — **WEB:** www.gogichicago.com
▧ Dinner nightly   **PRICE:** $$

HERB 😊

Thai

✗✗ | BYO◻   **MAP:** E3

In the sea of Thai restaurants that flank this area, elegant Herb stands out for its lovely wood and stone décor, and service staff friendly enough to use your name. This is killer Thai, elevated and prepared with care.

Herb offers both a three- and six-course prix-fixe dinner at tremendous value, but Chef/owner Patty Neumson's cooking is light (and delicious) enough to go the distance. A sample menu might begin with a cool pile of crunchy green papaya, carrot, and cucumber, laced in a beautifully balanced lime dressing with crispy vermicelli noodles and peanuts. Then move on to tofu and kabocha in a deliciously complex coconut curry full of wilted basil and heat. Soft glass noodles find their match in sautéed onions, fresh crab, and crunchy shrimp.

▧ 5424 N. Broadway (bet. Balmoral & Catalpa Aves.)
🚇 Bryn Mawr
℘ (773) 944-9050 — **WEB:** www.herbrestaurant.com
▧ Dinner Thu – Sun   **PRICE:** $$

GOOSEFOOT ❀

Contemporary

XX | ♿ BYO⯈

MAP: B5

This understated plate-glass façade may seem lost in a sea of mediocrity, but the restaurant it houses is truly distinct. The soothing décor appears minimal, with splashes of orange from the seating, bare tables, and Rodin replicas to fashion a space that is instantly likeable. A small painting purchased by the Chef and his wife on their honeymoon in Italy graces one corner of the room. Dishes are intricate and take time to be described, which may explain the relatively slow pace of dining here.

The menu showcases classical edge and contemporary artistry. Start with a melt-in-your-mouth lobster tail puddled in citrus beurre blanc, studded with tapioca pearls. Delicate, handmade tortellini are packed with maitake mushrooms and lovingly enhanced with fresh mint and shaved Perigord truffles. This may be followed by a slice of consommé-poached beef filet, pan-seared to medium-rare perfection and paired with enoki mushrooms, nasturtium purée, and drizzled with California olive oil.

Just when you think it couldn't possibly get any sweeter, the Goosefoot experience ends with handcrafted chocolates, a packet of seeds for your garden, and a warm sendoff from Chef Chris Nugent and his wife, Nina.

▨ 2656 W. Lawrence Ave. (bet. Talman & Washtenaw Aves.)
🚇 Rockwell
☎ (773) 942-7547 — **WEB:** www.goosefoot.net
▨ Dinner Wed – Sat

PRICE: $$$$

HOPLEAF 🐾
Gastropub

X | 🍺 ♿ ⛱ 🖥️

There are so many things to love about Chicago's taverns: their complete lack of attitude; their undying hospitality; and their downright delicious cooking.

Hopleaf is a classic example of all that and more, still packing the house 25 years after opening. A traditional bar graces the front, but the glassed-in kitchen is where the magic happens. Named after a pale ale brewed in Malta, Hopleaf fittingly flaunts a beer list so long that it's been called "a novel." It's hard to go wrong at this beloved gastropub, but don't miss the mussels if they're available. Another gem: the wood-grilled Duroc pork chop—a thick, juicy chop in a red wine glaze, set over white grits with smoky Gouda, and accompanied by roasted cauliflower and broccoli salsify.

▪ 5148 N. Clark St. (bet. Foster Ave. & Winona St.)
🚇 Berwyn
📞 (773) 334-9851 — **WEB:** www.hopleaf.com
▪ Lunch & dinner daily   PRICE: $$

JIN JU 🍴
Korean

X | 🖥️

A sexy spot on a bustling stretch of North Clark, Jin Ju spins out luscious Korean classics with aplomb. Inside, dim lighting, dark wood furnishings, and luxuriant fuchsia-red walls create a sophisticated coziness, while servers are gracious and attentive.

A simply named house salad showcases the restaurant's modern, accessible Korean ethos, combining meaty pan-seared portobello strips atop delicately bitter green leaf lettuce, torn sesame leaves, cucumbers, and scallions in a funky garlic-soy sauce. Without tableside barbecue grills, fatty pork slabs are sautéed in the kitchen for sweetly caramelized samgyupsal. Wrapped in sesame leaves with Brussels sprouts, beets, crispy leeks, and a smear of kicky miso paste, the package provides instant gratification.

▪ 5203 N. Clark St. (at Foster Ave.)
🚇 Berwyn
📞 (773) 334-6377 — **WEB:** www.jinjurestaurant.com
▪ Dinner Tue – Sun   PRICE: $$

JIN THAI 😋

Thai

✗ | 🛖 BYO

MAP: E3

In-the-know locals fill up on tasty Thai at this sleek corner hot spot, whose curving glass windows beckon many a passerby with views of and aromas from vibrant curries and spicy laab. Inside, a row of splashy pillows lends color and comfort to a wooden banquette, and woven placemats dress up dark wood tables.

Start a meal with zingy miang kham, a chopped mix of dried shrimp, fresh ginger, lime, peanuts, and coconut, all wrapped in a betel leaf. From there, move on to hot curry catfish or Sukothai noodle soup teeming with minced pork and steaming broth (add pinches of warm spices from the accompanying condiment tray for an even more soul-satisfying slurp). For dessert, pick from either roti ice cream, wonton bananas, or warm Thai custard.

▦ 5458 N. Broadway (at Catalpa Ave.)
🚇 Bryn Mawr
✆ (773) 681-0555 — **WEB:** www.jinthaicuisine.com
▦ Lunch & dinner Wed – Mon

PRICE: 😋

LUELLA'S SOUTHERN KITCHEN 😋

Southern

✗ | ♿ 🛋 BYO

MAP: C5

Luella's is named for Chef Darnell Reed's Southern-born great-grandmother, and for good reason: one bite of this soul-infused fare will transport you to her hometown of Morgan City, Mississippi, a place she left behind for Chicago many years ago—and one that lives on in her grandson's cooking. The no-frills, order-at-the-counter spot is simply adorned with genuinely welcoming service that only adds to the charm.

Every spoonful of Luella's andouille and chicken gumbo is one to remember, thanks to a roux that's been cooked for five (count 'em) hours. The hot, sugary beignets are a pastry wonder, and chicken and waffles drizzled with Bourbon syrup are Southern by way of Brussels, featuring thick, eggy Liège waffles standing in for the usual rounds.

▦ 4609 N. Lincoln Ave. (bet. Eastwood & Wilson Aves.)
🚇 Western (Brown)
✆ (773) 961-8196 — **WEB:** www.luellassouthernkitchen.com
▦ Lunch Tue – Sun   Dinner nightly

PRICE: $$

MANGO PICKLE 😌

Indian

✕

After nearly a decade spent traveling across India with her husband, Nakul Patel, Chef Marisa Paolillo was sufficiently inspired to return stateside and open a restaurant that celebrates its culinary diversity. Named for the country's most popular condiment, everything in Mango Pickle—from the colorful artwork and accessories to the richly layered curries—honors a deep appreciation for the South Asian country.

While dishes here riff on the classics, there are flavorful surprises at every turn. The creamy tomato-onion sauce of butter chicken is ramped up with earthy mushrooms and sundried tomatoes for a Mediterranean twist. Chana masala is spiked with ginger and garlic confit, and cod siolim kalwamche boasts a heady aroma of star anise and fennel.

▨ 5842 N. Broadway (bet. Rosedale Ave. & Victoria St.)
🚉 Thorndale
✆ (773) 944-5555 — **WEB:** www.mangopicklechicago.com
▨ Dinner Wed – Sun   **PRICE: $$**

PEARL'S SOUTHERN COMFORT 🍴🍽

Southern

✕✕ | 🍺 ⚿ 🏠 🛋

MAP: E3

Chicago's been on a Southern food kick of late, and this sparkling Andersonville charmer is a straight up hepcat. Its enormous arched windows open up to a completely revamped 100 year-old room, featuring long exposed ceiling beams, whitewashed brick, dark slate walls, and soft leather chairs.

But even with all that design swag, the main draw at Pearl's Southern Comfort is still the food. For starters, there's the ace barbecue, but guests should hardly stop there. Try the enormous double cut pork chop, grilled to supple perfection and paired with "dirty" farro salad, Cajun slaw, and pork jus. Another staple, the Louisiana jambalaya, is served decadently dark and spicy, brimming with tender chicken, Andouille sausage, and Crystal hot sauce.

▨ 5352 N. Broadway (bet. Balmoral & Berwyn Aves.)
🚉 Berwyn
✆ (773) 754-7419 — **WEB:** www.pearlschicago.com
▨ Lunch Sat – Sun   Dinner nightly   **PRICE: $$**

PHO 777 ⅈ○

Vietnamese

🍴

MAP: E4

A market's worth of fresh ingredients allows Pho 777 to stand out in a neighborhood where Vietnamese restaurants—and their signature soup—seem to populate every storefront. Bottles of hot sauce, jars of fiery condiments, and canisters of spoons and chopsticks clustered on each table make it easy for regulars to sit down and start slurping.

Add choices like meatballs, tendon, flank steak, and tofu to the cardamom- ginger- and clove-spiced beef broth, which fills a vat large enough to sate a lumberjack-sized appetite. Then throw in jalapeños, Thai basil, and mint to your liking. If you're not feeling like pho this time around, snack on spring rolls with house-made roasted peanut sauce; or a stack of lacy bánh xèo stuffed with pork, chili sauce and sprouts.

🏛 1063-65 W. Argyle St. (bet. Kenmore & Winthrop Aves.)
🚇 Argyle
📞 (773) 561-9909 — **WEB:** N/A
🍽 Lunch & dinner Tue – Sun

PRICE: 😊

PHO XE TANG - TANK NOODLE ⅈ○

Vietnamese

🍴 | ♿ BYO⊐

MAP: E4

A stone's throw from the Little Saigon EL, this simple corner spot keeps pho enthusiasts coming back for more. Communal cafeteria-style tables, crowded during prime meal times, are stocked with all the necessary funky and spicy condiments. Efficient service keeps the joint humming and lets the patrons focus on slurping.

Pho is the definitive draw here, and this fragrant, five-spiced, rice noodle- and beef-filled broth is accompanied by sprouts, lime wedges, and plenty of basil. Other delights on the massive menu include shrimp- and pork-stuffed rice flour rolls with addictive spicy and sour nuoc cham. Follow that with a fiery catfish soup simmered with an intriguing combination of okra, pineapple, and bamboo shoots drizzled with garlic oil.

🏛 4953-55 N. Broadway (at Argyle St.)
🚇 Argyle
📞 (773) 878-2253 — **WEB:** www.tank-noodle.com
🍽 Lunch & dinner Thu – Tue

PRICE: 😊

RAS DASHEN ⚫

Ethiopian

✂ | 🍺 & ⬜
MAP: E2

If you're lucky, grab a stool at one of the mossab tables to relish this Ethiopian kitchen's authentic cooking. Walls splashed with rust-orange and rattan chairs further elevate the faithful appeal, while a bar pouring honey wine and African beers keeps the local community happy.

Collective trays with delicacies speed out of the kitchen, so those who wish to immerse themselves in this nation's culinary culture should begin—on a light note—with Zenash's salad tossing chickpeas and crispy shallots with a touch of vinegar and tons of toasty spices. Gored gored highlights brisket marinated with awaze; and yebeg alicha is an aromatic lamb stew complete with spicy veggies. Sides of spongy and tart injera are ideal for cooling the palate from the creeping heat.

▦ 5846 N. Broadway (bet. Ardmore & Thorndale Aves.)
🏛 Thorndale
☎ (773) 506-9601 — **WEB:** www.rasdashenchicago.com
▦ Lunch & dinner Wed – Mon   **PRICE:** $$

SABRI NIHARI 🐭

Indian

✕✕ | &
MAP: C1

Sabri Nihari outshines the restaurant competition on this crowded stretch of West Devon Avenue. Make your way inside the expansive and massively posh Indo-Pakistani spot, where crystal chandeliers make gold-hued walls gleam more brightly.

As with many Southeast Asian restaurants, vegetarian dishes abound—but that's only the beginning of the diverse menu. Whole okra pods add a grassy, peppery bite to beefy bhindi gosht, and delightful chicken charga, an entire spatchcocked bird marinated in yogurt and lime, is rubbed generously with spices before crisping up in the deep fryer. No alcohol is served in deference to many of the abstaining clientele, but you won't miss it; buttery naan and creamy lassi with homemade yogurt help to balance out the spice-fest.

▦ 2500-2502 W. Devon Ave. (at Campbell Ave.)
☎ (773) 465-3272 — **WEB:** www.sabrinihari.com
▦ Lunch & dinner daily   **PRICE:** 🪙

SAN SOO GAB SAN 😊

Korean

✗

Tucked into a tiny strip mall in the West Edgewater-Upper Andersonville area, San Soo Gab San has generated quite a buzz among serious Korean food fans. Inside, you'll find a warm, welcoming space with large tabletop grills to cook your own meats.

Most excitingly, the authentic, traditional dishes turned out of the kitchen don't bow or cater to Western sensibilities—to wit, an incredibly flavorful bowl of piping hot goat meat soup arrives with wild sesame green leaves and a flutter of seeds. Among the many popular casseroles and stews, don't miss the beo seot danjan zigae, choc-a-block with tender tofu, savory mushrooms, beef and veggies. The delicious barbecue is perfect for a group feast or those looking to have some fun with their food.

■ 5247 N. Western Ave. (at Berwyn Ave.)
🚇 Western (Brown)
✆ (773) 334-1589 — **WEB:** www.sansoogabsan.com
■ Lunch & dinner daily   **PRICE:** $$

TASTE OF PERU 🍴

Peruvian

✗ | BYO🍷

Tucked inside a strip mall and entirely plain-Jane in appearance, foodies trek to this caliente fave for a formidable meal of authentic dishes. The owner is chatty and tunes groovy, all of which make for a wonderful precursor to such peppery items as aji de gallina (shredded chicken in a walnut sauce, enriched with parmesan) or chupe de camarones (a hot, spicy, bright bowl of shrimp and rice). This is clearly not the place for a pisco sour, but feels like Sundays con la familia where papa a la huancaina doused in amarillo chile, and arroz chaufa with veggies and beef jerky-like strips are merely some of the items on offer.

It's worth noting though that while the food is decidedly traditional, mysteriously there's no pork to be found anywhere on the menu.

■ 6545 N. Clark St. (bet. Albion & Arthur Aves.)
✆ (773) 381-4540 — **WEB:** www.tasteofperu.com
■ Lunch & dinner daily   **PRICE:** ☜

VINCENT ⚭

Belgian

✗✗ | 🏠 ⚮

MAP: E3

Go Dutch at Vincent, where innovative yet approachable cooking meets a tried-and-true European bistro menu, boasting enough cheese to satisfy even the pickiest turophile. Adding to the romance, high-top marble tables and brocade-papered walls make for a warm, intimate ambience that's accented by tall votive candles.

Got an appetite? An overflowing pot of P.E.I. mussels is a decadent meal on its own, brimming with bits of pork belly, chilies, scallions, and cilantro, accompanied by a big bowl of traditional frites with mayonnaise. Basil and lemon balsam perk up risotto with charred purple cauliflower and braised fennel. Also, you'll want to hold on to your fork for slices of lemon butter cake with Chantilly cream and blueberry compote.

▨ 1475 W. Balmoral Ave. (bet. Clark St. & Glenwood Ave.)
🚇 Berwyn
✆ (773) 334-7168 — **WEB:** www.vincentchicago.com
▨ Lunch Sat – Sun   Dinner Tue – Sun

PRICE: $$

CHICAGO ▶ ANDERSONVILLE, EDGEWATER & UPTOWN

The sun is out — let's eat alfresco!
Look for 🏠.

BUCKTOWN & WICKER PARK

UKRANIAN VILLAGE · WEST TOWN

A CAVE OF COOL

Like many of the Windy City's neighborhoods, Bucktown and Wicker Park have seen their residents shift from waves of Polish immigrants and wealthy businessmen who've erected stately mansions on Hoyne and Pierce avenues, to those young, hip crowds introducing modern taquerias and craft breweries to these streets. Still, the neighborhood knows how to retain its trendsetting rep, and continues to draw those who crave to be on the cutting edge of all things creative, contemporary, and culinary. Far from the internationally known boutiques along Magnificent Mile, indie

shops and artisan producers of Milwaukee and Damen avenues offer one-of-a-kind treasures for all the five senses. Get a taste of Wicker Park's vast underground music scene at Reckless Records or at some of the city's largest music events, including the Wicker Park Fest, which is held each July and features no less than 28 bands. Likewise, the annual Green Music Fest draws every eco-minded resident around. Snap up funky home accessories and original works at flea market-chic Penguin Foot Pottery, or wear art on your sleeve by designing your own Tee at the appropriately named T-shirt Deli.

HOT DOGS AND HAUTE TREATS

It's a well-known saying that you don't want to know how the sausage is made, but the person who coined this phrase clearly never tasted the bounty from **Vienna Beef Factory**. Their popular workshop tour leaves visitors yearning for a 1/3-pound Mike Ditka Polish sausage at the café, or even a make-your-own-Chicago-dog kit with celery salt, sport peppers, and electric-green pickle relish from the gift shop. For more Eastern European fun, **Rich's Deli** is Ukrainian Village's go-to market for copious cuts of smoked pork as well as *kabanosy*, *pasztet*, Polish vodka, and Slavic mustard among other terrific stuff.

Unlike many local emporiums in town, the staff here is fluent in English, so don't be afraid to make your inquiries. All other lingering questions on meat may be answered after talking with husband-and-wife team, Rob and Allie Levitt, the brains (and stomachs) behind Noble Square's **The Butcher & Larder**. Combining the growing interest in whole animal butchery and a desire

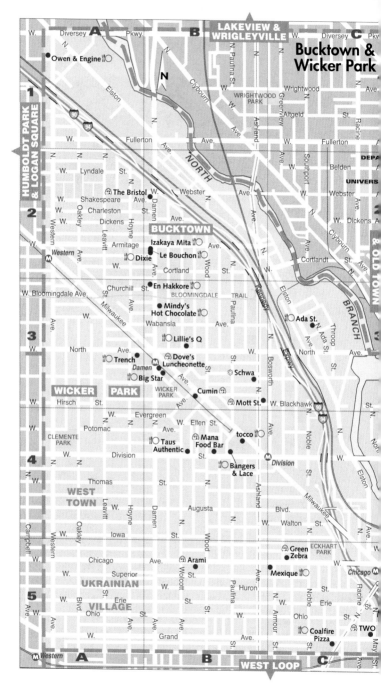

W. Diversey Pkwy. **A** **B** W. Diversey Pkwy. **C**

Owen & Engine ⫯◯

Elston Ave.

N. Clybourn Ave.

N. Paulina St.

Wrightwood Ave.

WRIGHTWOOD
PARK

Greenview

Altgeld St.

Racine

1

HUMBOLDT PARK & LOGAN SQUARE

W. Fullerton Ave.

N. Ashland Ave.

Southport

W. Fullerton

DEPA

UNIVERS

W. Lyndale St.

W. Webster Ave.

W. Belden

W. Webster

& OLD TOWN

2

The Bristol ⊕

W. Shakespeare Ave.

W. Charleston St.

W. Oakley

W. Dickens St.

N. Damen

Hoyne

N. Leavitt

N. Western Ave.

Ⓜ Western

N.

N.

W. Armitage Ave.

BUCKTOWN

Izakaya Mita ⫯◯

⫯◯ Dixie

Le Bouchon ⫯◯

Wood St.

W. Cortland St.

Clybourn

Cortlandt

Elston Ave.

Kennedy Expwy.

Throop St.

BRANCH

Churchill St.

W. Bloomingdale Ave.

En Hakkore ⫯◯

BLOOMINGDALE TRAIL

Paulina St.

Ada St. ●

N. Ada St.

Milwaukee Ave.

Mindy's
Hot Chocolate ⫯◯

Wabansia Ave.

W. North Ave.

Bosworth

3

W. North Ave.

⫯◯ Trench ●

Damen

Lillie's Q ⫯◯

⊕ Dove's
Luncheonette

Ⓜ

⫯◯ Big Star ●

WICKER
PARK

Cumin ⊕

✿ Schwa

W. Blackhawk

Hoyne

94

W. Hirsch St.

⊕ Mott St. ●

N.

W. Evergreen Ave.

W. Ellen St.

Noble

WICKER PARK

W. Potomac

CLEMENTE
PARK

⫯◯ Taus
Authentic ●

⊕ Mana
Food Bar

tocco ⫯◯ ●

Elston

4

N.

W. Division St.

⫯◯ Bangers
& Lace

Ⓜ Division

W.

Milwaukee Ave.

**WEST
TOWN**

W. Thomas St.

Leavitt

Hoyne

Damen

W. Augusta

Ashland Ave.

Blvd.

W. Walton St.

Campbell

Oakley

Western

W. Iowa St.

Wood

ECKHART
PARK

⊕ Green
Zebra ●

Noble

W. Chicago Ave.

⊕ Arami ●

Wolcott

Paulina St.

Mexique ⫯◯ ●

Ⓜ Chicago

Racine

UKRAINIAN

W. Superior St.

St.

5

W. Erie St.

VILLAGE

W. Ohio St.

W. Erie St.

Armour

⫯◯ Coalfire
Pizza ●

⊕ TWO

Ⓜ Western **A** W. Grand Ave. **B** **WEST LOOP** **C** May

to support local farmers, the Levitts showcase sausages, terrines, and house-cured bacon, while also conducting demos on how to break down a side of beef. If God is indeed in the details, then marketplace extraordinaire, **Goddess & Grocer**, brings to life this turn of phrase. While its vast selection of items may be the stuff of dreams among snooty gourmands and top chefs, even novices can be found here, stocking up on

soups, salads, and chili—better than what Mom used to make back in the day. They also cater, so go ahead and pretend like you crafted those delicate dinner party hors d'oeuvres all on your own!

SUGAR RUSH

A spectrum of hand-crafted goodies make this region a rewarding destination for anyone addicted to sweet. For nearly a century, family-run **Margie's Candies** has been hand-dipping its chocolate bonbons and serving towering scoops of homemade ice cream to those Logan Square denizens and dons (including Al Capone, that old softy). Equally retro in attitude, the lip-smacking seasonal slices and small-town vibe of **Hoosier Mama Pie Company** brings old-timey charm to this stretch of Chicago Avenue. From tiered wedding cakes to replicas of Wrigley Field recreated in batter and frosting, a tempting selection of desserts is displayed in the window at **Alliance Bakery** and would make even Willy Wonka green with envy. But, if you're looking for something

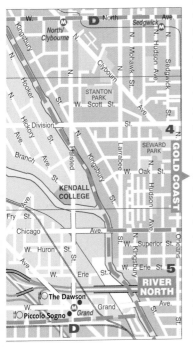

a little less traditional, unusual combinations are the norm at **Black Dog Gelato**, where goat cheese, cashew, and caramel come together for a uniquely satisfying scoop.

SUDS AND SPUDS

The craft beer movement has been brewing in Chicagoland for some time now, where lovers of quality suds and superlative bar snacks find an impressive listing of both in Bucktown and Wicker Park. Regulars at Logan Square's **Revolution Brewing** snack on bacon-fat popcorn and sweet potato cakes while sipping on the in-house Double Fist Pale Ale or Anti-Hero IPA. This holy union between food and beer is always reaching epic heights at **Piece**, which not only serves up one of Chicagoland's most popular hand-tossed pizzas but also produces a roster of award-winning beers to accompany its crusty New Haven-style pies. And, for a master class on the wide and wonderful world of craft brews, the noted beer school at Wicker Park's **Map Room** gives students a greater appreciation for the art—though a self-taught tour of the bar's worldwide selection is quite educational and perhaps more enjoyable?

THE LUSH LIFE

However, if south-of-the-border eats are what you need, then head on over to **Taco & Burrito Express #3**. This fast, family-run, and cash-only spot doles out delicious al pastor tacos until the party winds down—at 11:00 P.M. For those who prefer their food brought to them by *luchadores* donning wrestling masks, cool and quirky **Tamale Spaceship** truck

is yet another fixture here, in the form of a brick and mortar storefront. Sports of another sort grab the spotlight at **Emporium Arcade Bar** where rows of video games and pinball machines from the 1980s bring back memories for those who grew up hitting the arcade. And this of course becomes even more fun when paired with a craft beer or whiskey shot.

KITCHEN SKILLS

Meals at **Kendall College Dining Room** let you brag about knowing future Michelin-starred chefs before they've hit it big. As one of Chicago's premier culinary institutions, this college gives its chef trainees real-world guidance by way of elegant lunch and dinner service. Floor-to-ceiling windows overlook the professional kitchen, where instructors can be seen helping students fine-tune their fine dining skills. Reservations are required, but the experience is a must for home cooks looking to be inspired. For a more hands-on affair, classes at **Cooking Fools** let aspiring

Food Network stars hone their knife skills or prepare a batch of tamales from scratch. Feeling the need to flaunt your culinary credentials over a dinner party at home? Simply swing by the **Wicker Park & Bucktown Farmer's Market** (open on Sundays) and stock your pantry with an impressive fleet of fresh produce, artisanal cheeses, and much, much more. Afterwards, you can always peruse the shelves of **Olivia's Market** for painstakingly sourced specialty items, as well as a massive wine and beer selection. Then drop by **LocalFolks Foods**, a family-run enterprise whose chief mission is to develop natural gourmet condiments (mustard and hot sauce anyone?) for slathering over hearty burgers or dogs. You may also purchase these same delightful treats from the lauded **Green Grocer** and make your next cookout the envy of everyone on the block. Finally, feel ready to grow your own vegetables? Sign up for a plot at **Frankie Machine Community Garden** and see if you've got a green thumb!

Segment left margin vertical text:

ADA ST. 🍴

Contemporary

🗙 | 🍸 ♿ 🏛 ⊡

MAP: C3

Despite its obscure location among the industrial warehouses of far-east Wicker Park, adventurous diners have no trouble seeking out Ada St. Reservations aren't accepted here after 6:30 P.M., so the cozy, brick-walled lounge quickly becomes a party space where patrons peruse the wooden cubbies of vinyl to create their own soundtrack.

The menu of small plates takes influence from hearty gastropub dishes, as in the hangar steak plated with smoked potatoes and salsa verde; but the inspiration doesn't stop there. Luscious burrata dabbed with mint and walnut pesto entices with a Mediterranean accent, while tequila-glazed grilled octopus reflects the penchant for Latin American flavors of this kitchen's newly installed executive chef.

🔲 1664 N. Ada St. (bet. Concord Pl. & Wabansia Ave.)
☎ (773) 697-7069 — **WEB:** www.adastreetchicago.com
🔲 Dinner Tue – Sun

PRICE: $$

ARAMI 😊

Japanese

🗙 | 🍶 ♿

MAP: B5

Come to this bamboo-clad izakaya, with its comfortable sushi bar and soaring skylights, for impressively rendered small plates and specialty cocktails featuring Japanese spirits. The night's tsukemono can reveal spicy okra, crisp hearts of palm, and sweet burdock root. The nigiri selection might showcase New Zealand King salmon topped with pickled wasabi root. The robata produces grilled maitakes with Japanese sea salt and black garlic purée; and gani korroke, a crunchy-creamy crab croquette, is plated with togarashi-spiked mayonnaise.

Don't turn down the all-ice cream dessert menu, which includes enticing flavors like coconut-cinnamon-banana. It comes nestled in granola-like bits of miso-graham cracker crumble for a finish as sweet as it is unique.

🔲 1829 W. Chicago Ave. (bet. Wolcott Ave & Wood St.)
🚇 Division
☎ (312) 243-1535 — **WEB:** www.aramichicago.com
🔲 Dinner nightly

PRICE: $$

BANGERS & LACE 🍴

Gastropub

🍴 | 🍺 ♿ 🛋️   **MAP:** B4

Despite the frilly connotations, this sausage-and-beer mecca's name refers not to doilies, but to the delicate layers of foam that remain in the glass after your craft brew has been quaffed. You'll also have lots of opportunity to study the lace curtains as you plow through their extensive draft beer menu, noted on blackboards in the comfortably worn-in front bar room.

Decadent foie gras corn dogs (actually French garlic sausage wrapped with soft-sweet brioche cornbread) and veal brats with melted Gouda elevate the humble sausage; while a slew of sandwiches suit simpler tastes. Grilled cheese gilds the lily with taleggio, raclette, and Irish cheddar; and dreamy house-made chips drizzled with truffle oil and malt vinegar are more than a bar snack.

- 1670 W. Division St. (at Paulina St.)
- Damen (Blue)
- (773) 252-6499 — **WEB:** www.bangersandlacechicago.com
- Lunch Sat – Sun   Dinner nightly   **PRICE: $$**

BIG STAR 🍴

Mexican

🍴 | 🍹 ♿ 🏠 💵   **MAP:** B3

Bucktown's favorite taqueria has all the fixings for a fiesta. Craft beers, custom-bottled Bourbons, and pitchers of margaritas wash down the affordable abundance. And, despite the grungy décor, the vibe is as intoxicating as the aroma of the taco de chorizo verde. The patio is even more of a party, and sun-starved Chicagoans can be spotted out there soon after the groundhog has (or hasn't) seen his shadow.

Tacos are served individually, thus allowing ample opportunity to graze on the likes of the pollo pibil—achiote- and citrus-marinated chicken thighs steamed in banana leaves, topped with pickled onion slices and cilantro. Save room for the salsa de frijole con queso, a crock of pinto bean dip accompanied by lime salt-sprinkled tortilla chips.

- 1531 N. Damen Ave. (bet. Milwaukee & Wicker Park Aves.)
- Damen (Blue)
- (773) 235-4039 — **WEB:** www.bigstarchicago.com
- Lunch & dinner daily   **PRICE:** 🍴

THE BRISTOL 😀

American

✗✗ | 🍸 ♿ 🛋 🎴

MAP: B2

Get to know your neighbors a little better at this dim, bustling haunt boasting seasonal American fare with a Mediterranean twist. Regulars sit shoulder-to-shoulder at the concrete bar, squinting under filament bulbs to see the constantly changing menu's latest additions on chalkboards throughout the room.

Start with a Moscow Mule in a frosty copper mug to go with your head-on prawns a la plancha with anchovy butter and tarragon, or smoked whitefish dip with horseradish and saltines. Large plates sing with comfort, especially the Amish half-chicken with mustard-dill spaetzle and chicken jus. Weekend brunch is mighty popular, whether for the hangover-curing noodle bowl or plump cinnamon rolls. Homemade nutter butters remain an iconic finale.

🔲 2152 N. Damen Ave. (bet. Shakespeare & Webster Aves.)
📞 (773) 862-5555 — **WEB:** www.thebristolchicago.com
🔲 Lunch Sat – Sun   Dinner nightly

PRICE: $$

COALFIRE PIZZA 🍴

Pizza

✗

MAP: C5

Sure, you could come for a salad, but the focus here is on pizza—and yours should be, too. The cozy room features an open kitchen where pie production is on display for all to see. And in a playful bit of recycling, empty tomato sauce cans on each table become stands for sizzling pizzas churned straight from the 800-degree coal oven.

This hot spot has its ratio down to a fine art and knows not to burden its thin, crispy crust that's blackened and blistered in all the right places. The mortadella is a delight, with chopped garlic and gossamer slices of peppercorn-flecked sausage. Care to go your own way? Build the perfect pie with toppings that run the gamut from Gorgonzola to goat cheese.

A second location in Lakeview continues to thrive.

🔲 1321 W. Grand Ave. (bet. Ada & Elizabeth Sts.)
🚇 Chicago (Blue)
📞 (312) 226-2625 — **WEB:** www.coalfirechicago.com
🔲 Lunch Fri – Sun   Dinner Tue – Sun

PRICE: 🍝

CUMIN 😋

Indian

✕✕ | ♿   **MAP:** B3

This proudly run blend of Nepalese and Indian eats sits among a plethora of bars, coffee shops, and vintage stores in boho-centric Bucktown. While fans of the sub-continent love Cumin for its clean and modern surrounds, linen-lined tables struggle to contain the myriad plates that pile up during its ubiquitous lunch buffet.

Paintings of mountain scenes decorate crimson-red walls and prep diners for an authentic range of flavorful food hailing from the Himalayan frontier. Get gnawing on namche sekuwa or tandoori goat flecked with spices and paired with crunchy green peppers. Then soak up pieces of buttery naan in a hearty vegetarian stew (aalu tama bodi) combining potatoes, bamboo shoots and black eyed peas. Cool things down with sweet and milky mango kulfi.

▨ 1414 N. Milwaukee Ave. (bet. Evergreen & Wolcott Aves.)
▨ Damen (Blue)
✆ (773) 342-1414 — **WEB:** www.cumin-chicago.com
▨ Lunch Tue – Sun   Dinner nightly   **PRICE:** 💰💰

THE DAWSON 🍴

Gastropub

✕✕ | 🍸 ♿ 🏡 🖥 🛋 📖   **MAP:** D5

The Dawson has everything you can ask for in a gastropub—a convivial vibe, clever bites, and great libations. The Surfer Rosa for instance (with tequila, mezcal, blood orange and chilies) serves to loosen up diners jonesing for big flavors. Inside, globe lights shine like beacons through the façade's lofty windows. And, a wraparound bar attracts spirited guests like moths to a flame. A communal table and open kitchen with counter offer multiple opportunities for meeting, greeting, and eating.

When hunger strikes, caramelized onion sabayon, potato confit, and garlicky pea shoots add depth to Arctic char. And lest you forget dessert, Bourbon-pecan bread pudding with flash-frozen vanilla cream and sea salt-butterscotch sauce, is meant for sharing—or not.

▨ 730 W. Grand Ave. (at Halsted St.)
▨ Chicago (Blue)
✆ (312) 243-8955 — **WEB:** www.the-dawson.com
▨ Lunch Sat – Sun   Dinner nightly   **PRICE:** $$

41

DIXIE 🍴

Southern

XX | 🍸 🛏️

From the brightly whitewashed exterior to the freshly installed porch area complete with rocking chairs, the Southern-styled redo of the old Takashi space is everything you'd expect from Chef—and South Carolina native—Charlie McKenna (also of Lillie's Q). Despite the somewhat curious absence of antebellum style and slow drawls, this cozily arranged interior is luminous, chic, and charming. And then there's the bar of course, which proffers a great Bourbon listing and impressive cocktails that may include a vintage Boulevardier.

The glassed-in kitchen, where the team is sharply accented with indigo-hued aprons, turns out a roster of updated down-home cooking. And while the flavors are familiar, the execution here is actually quite modern— envision pan-seared catfish with succotash and foamy harissa nage.

▦ 1952 N. Damen Ave. (bet. Armitage Ave. & Homer St.)
🚇 Damen (Blue)
✆ (773) 688-4466 — **WEB:** www.dixiechicago.com
▦ Lunch Sat – Sun   Dinner Wed – Sun

PRICE: $$

DOVE'S LUNCHEONETTE 😊

American

X | 🍱

With a chill, throwback vibe, all-day breakfast, and a drink list with more than 70 labels of agave spirits, this One Off Hospitality roadhouse is a Wicker Park hipster's dream come true. To drive the point home, the diner features wood-paneled walls, counter seating, a record player spinning the blues, and of course, Tex-Mex fare listed on a wall-mounted letter board. The daily special may be a blueberry quinoa pancake, while savory favorites include crunchy buttermilk fried chicken with chorizo verde gravy or the farmer's cheese-stuffed Anaheim chile relleno, served in a pool of tomato-serrano sauce with pasilla chiles and pickled chayote slices.

Pies from Hoosier Mama Pie Co. are a grand finale; try the lemony Atlantic Beach with a saltine crust.

▦ 1545 N. Damen Ave. (bet. Milwaukee & Pierce Aves.)
🚇 Damen (Blue)
✆ (773) 645-4060 — **WEB:** www.doveschicago.com
▦ Lunch & dinner daily

PRICE: $$

EN HAKKORE ¶◯

Korean

✗

Healthy doesn't have to be humdrum. This simple little Korean eatery, run by a husband-and-wife team and decorated with more than a hint of whimsy, specializes in big bowls of bibimbap. You choose your rice and protein, be it pork or barbecue beef, decide on the heat level and then dive straight in—up to 16 different vegetables are used and they're as tasty as they are colorful. Also worth trying are the steamed mandoo (pork dumplings) and the curiously addictive tacos made with paratha.

Simply place your order at the counter, grab a plastic fork and, if you're with friends, commandeer the large communal table. There's no alcohol (and it's not BYOB) so instead take advantage of an invigorating soft drink from the fridge. You'll feel so virtuous.

▪ 1840 N. Damen Ave. (bet. Churchill & Moffat Sts.)
▪ Damen (Blue)
✆ (773) 772-9880 — **WEB:** N/A
▪ Lunch & dinner Mon – Sat

PRICE: ⊛

GREEN ZEBRA ☺

Vegetarian

XX | 🍸 ♿ 🍽

Named after the popular heirloom tomato, Chef/owner Shawn McClain's vegetarian standby is beloved among Chicagoans looking for an upscale meat-free experience. The dining room's minimalist décor is sleek and soothing, all earthy brown hues and potted greenery. The kitchen's offerings keep the omnivore palate interested by weaving in a world of influences, while the small plates conceit allows diners to freely explore a variety of this skillful cuisine.

Tomato rasam soup is a nod to India frilled with roasted eggplant and lentils, just as kimchi-and-tofu potstickers with black garlic soy sauce display influences farther east. The highly satisfying za'atar-roasted acorn squash is composed with a black kale- and chickpea-flour cobbler.

▪ 1460 W. Chicago Ave. (at Greenview Ave.)
▪ Chicago (Blue)
✆ (312) 243-7100 — **WEB:** www.greenzebrachicago.com
▪ Dinner Tue – Sun

PRICE: $$

IZAKAYA MITA ⅋○

Japanese

✗ | 🍸

MAP: B2

This Bucktown addition is a family-run tavern worth seeking out for its homespun take on izakaya eats and gracious hospitality.

Start with single-serve sake in a jar so cute you'll want to smuggle it home, or a cocktail inspired by Japanese literature (the Norwegian Wood, a delicious interpretation of the Haruki Murakami novel blends whiskey, Luxardo, sweet vermouth, and orange bitters). The array of small plates brims with creativity and flavor: tsukune are coarse-ground, delightfully chewy, and achieve a mouthwateringly charred exterior from having been grilled over bincho-tan; while tako-yaki are as delicious as any found on a Tokyo street cart. Korroke, a panko-crusted potato croquette, comes with tonkatsu sauce for delicious dunking.

▦ 1960 N. Damen Ave. (at Armitage Ave.)
🚇 Western (Blue)
✆ (773) 799-8677 — **WEB:** www.izakayamita.com
▦ Lunch Sat – Sun   Dinner nightly   **PRICE:** 🍴

LE BOUCHON ⅋○

French

✗

MAP: B2

Pressed-tin ceilings? Check. Brick-and-Dijon color scheme? Of course. Le Bouchon proffers the quintessential bistro experience, where straightforward French cooking never goes out of style and the regulars keep returning for more. The informal atmosphere gets convivially raucous as the night goes on with thirsty and hungry hordes lining the bar and petite dining room.

Over in the kitchen, familiar and approachable favorites rule the menu: soupe à l'oignon, wearing its traditional topper of broiled Gruyère on a moist crouton, oozes and bubbles over the sides of a ramekin. And an ample fillet of saumon poché napped in beurre blanc is the very essence of simplicity.

A lunch prix-fixe keeps the wallet light but belly full.

▦ 1958 N. Damen Ave. (at Armitage Ave.)
🚇 Damen (Blue)
✆ (773) 862-6600 — **WEB:** www.lebouchonofchicago.com
▦ Lunch & dinner Mon – Sat   **PRICE:** $$

LILLIE'S Q ⑪🍴

Barbecue

✗✗ | 🍹 🍺 ♿ ⛱   **MAP:** B3

Bucktown's urban barbecue shack takes a scholarly approach to 'cue, as each table bears a caddy stocked with six regionally specific sauces for embellishing the slow-smoked meats to come. Cocktails served in Mason jars are a specialty made from "moonshine" offered at three proof levels, and servers in modern mechanic's shirts tend to the crowds clamoring for heaps of smoked meats rubbed in "Carolina dirt." Tri-tip is tender and pink-tinged after its time in the smoker with the joint's signature dry rub; while the succulent smoked hot link rests in a butter-griddled, top-sliced brioche bun served with Southern-style coleslaw.

And if at-home grilling is your thing, you'll be pleased to know that the mouthwatering sauces are available by mail order.

🟦 1856 W. North Ave. (at Wolcott Ave.)
🚇 Damen (Blue)
📞 (773) 772-5500 — **WEB:** www.lilliesq.com
🟦 Lunch & dinner daily   **PRICE: $$**

MANA FOOD BAR 😊

Vegetarian

✗ | ♿ ⛱   **MAP:** B4

Feeling like your body needs a jump-start? Mana, whose name translates to "the life force coursing through nature," is a good place to get your mojo back. Though welcoming to vegans, vegetarians, gluten-free diners, and anyone who's looking for a nutrient boost, it's not just health food: the small space also offers a full bar with sake cocktails, smoothies, and freshly squeezed juices.

Mana may be a tiny spot, but its diverse menu of vegetarian dishes is big on taste—and spice. Korean bibimbap mixes a roster of vegetables like pea pods, roasted carrots, and pickled daikon with a fresh sunny side-up egg; while horseradish and cracked black pepper sneak into macaroni and cheese. House-made hot sauce with serranos and jalapeños adds extra pep to any dish.

🟦 1742 W. Division St. (bet. Paulina & Wood Sts.)
🚇 Division
📞 (773) 342-1742 — **WEB:** www.manafoodbar.com
🟦 Lunch Sat   Dinner nightly   **PRICE:** 😊

MEXIQUE ¶○

Mexican

XX | &

Large groups fill most of the banquettes in this slender space, but a bar stretching half the length of the room makes it easy for smaller parties to stop in for a sip of sangria. A rear window offers a glimpse of Chef Carlos Gaytan at work in the kitchen, and congratulatory graffiti from visiting chefs provides a fun distraction on the way to the restroom.

While the chef's French-leaning dishes seem to have meandered too far from their Mexican soul, his cooking skills and hybrid approach still remain impressive. Take the delightful pescamal that sits in a pool of puréed black bean sauce humming with perfect heat; or cordero, which reveals lamb chops with a ruby-red center and salty feta. Vanilla ice cream and fresh berries finish a fine chocolate fondant.

 1529 W. Chicago Ave. (bet. Armour St. & Ashland Ave.)
 Chicago (Blue)
 (312) 850-0288 — WEB: www.jbandala.mx/mexique
 Lunch & dinner Tue – Sun

PRICE: $$

MINDY'S HOT CHOCOLATE ¶○

Contemporary

XX | &

Bucktown wouldn't be the same without this sweet spot run by pastry chef extraordinaire, Mindy Segal. Diners walk past decadent hot chocolate mix and cookies on display before hitting an industrial-chic space fitted with sleek dark wood, caramel-brown walls, and chocolate-toned leather banquettes.

Get the point yet? Decadent chocolate is the name of the game here, though guests will be delighted to discover savory items beyond their expectations. Try the roasted tomato soup, garnished with bright green onion slivers; or the BLT with pesto aïoli, heirloom tomato, avocado, and thick, crispy maple-cayenne bacon.

An affogato—a scoop of coffee-cocoa nib ice cream paired with the chef's namesake hot chocolate—makes for the perfect finale.

 1747 N. Damen Ave. (bet. St. Paul Ave. & Willow St.)
 Damen (Blue)
 (773) 489-1747 — WEB: www.hotchocolatechicago.com
 Lunch Wed – Sun   Dinner Tue – Sun

PRICE: $$

MOTT ST. 🐷

Fusion

✗ | 🍴 🏠 🛋

MAP: B3

New Yorkers know Mott St. as the bustling artery in the heart of Chinatown, but to Chicagoans the name connotes something off the beaten path. Inside the low-slung, stand-alone red structure, a chicken wire-caged pantry is stocked with jars of red pepper, black vinegar, and other pungent edibles—all of which appear again in the food on your plate.

Offerings at this hip haven crisscross the globe, melding diverse ingredients for an utterly unique dining experience. Shredded kohlrabi substitutes green papaya for a Thai-inspired salad tossed with candied shrimp, poached chicken, and plenty of fresh herbs. Stuffed cabbage bears a Korean accent with tender chunks of slow-braised pork, tangy Napa cabbage kimchi, and crunchy sticky rice.

▨ 1401 N. Ashland Ave. (at Blackhawk St.)
🚇 Division
✆ (773) 687-9977 — **WEB:** www.mottstreetchicago.com
▨ Lunch Sun   Dinner Tue – Sat

PRICE: $$

OWEN & ENGINE 🍴

Gastropub

✗✗ | 🍹 🍺 🛋

MAP: A1

Owen & Engine's charm extends from its glossy black façade into its warm polished wood interior and all the way to the second-floor dining room that sees action into the wee hours. Brocade wallpaper, gas lights, and studded leather club chairs lend a Victorian feel. A frequently changing draft list always features a few selections pulled from a beer cask (or "engine").

British-inspired gastropub grub matches the impressive roster of brews and Pimm's cups. Bar nibbles like mustard-glazed soft pretzels with Welsh rarebit for dipping; or peanuts tossed in sriracha, Worcestershire, and brown sugar cater to the snacking sort. Hearty entrées like bangers and mash feature house-made Slagel Family Farm's pork sausage and potatoes smothered in onion gravy.

▨ 2700 N. Western Ave. (at Schubert Ave.)
✆ (773) 235-2930 — **WEB:** www.owenengine.com
▨ Lunch Sat – Sun   Dinner nightly

PRICE: $$

PICCOLO SOGNO 🍴

Italian

✕✕ | 🍸 ♿ 🏠 🖼 🛎

In-the-know locals craving mouthwatering Italian fare head to this swanky spot, usually packed with a dressy crowd. Inside, they are welcomed by a palette of rich, cool hues, crystal-beaded light fixtures that hang overhead, and an open kitchen boasting a wood-burning oven.

Piccolo Sogno's rustic yet refined menu offers traditional dishes with a twist. A version of the ubiquitous beet salad (both red and golden) is elevated here by shaved fennel, a drizzle of bright citrus oil, and a dollop of creamy, lush buffalo milk ricotta. If you need further encouragement, let us recommend the rabbit. Braised in a white wine sauce redolent of rosemary and lemon, the tender meat is served with wilted escarole and porridge-like semolina pudding.

■ 464 N. Halsted St. (at Milwaukee Ave.)
🚇 Grand (Blue)
📞 (312) 421-0077 — **WEB:** www.piccolosognorestaurant.com
■ Lunch Mon – Fri   Dinner nightly   PRICE: $$

TAUS AUTHENTIC 🍴

International

✕✕ | 🍸 ♿ 🏠 🖼 🛏 🛎

You'll want to make an evening of it at this Wicker Park gem, where a stylish front lounge—complete with a working fireplace—makes for a cozy spot to enjoy a beer or cocktail. Then you may proceed to linger over a meal in the beautiful dining room, a modern vision of wood, powder blue velvet, and plate glass windows.

Chef Michael Taus has designed a menu made for grazing: think charcuterie, cheese, and starters including a sunchoke dosa. Made from lentils and basmati rice, this lacy crêpe is topped with bits of tender sunchokes in a spicy red curry sauce sweetened by golden raisins and candied pumpkin seeds. A tasting portion of pan-seared fluke, plated with sweet chili vinaigrette and a Korean-style pancake studded with dried shrimp, is equally delicious.

■ 1846 W. Division St. (bet. Marion Ct. & Wolcott Ave.)
🚇 Division
📞 (312) 561-4500 — **WEB:** www.tausauthentic.com
■ Lunch Sun   Dinner Tue – Sun   PRICE: $$

SCHWA ❀
Contemporary

🍴 | BYO

There comes a point when pared-down style jumps from being easy-to-miss and becomes hard-to-forget. When a utilitarian and self-consciously bare-bones interior becomes attractively modern and industrial. When a lack of any FOH staff makes the service seem playfully all-hands-on-deck. The explicit rap music playing in the background reflects the deeply talented chefs' ethos, going well beyond laissez-faire to reach the point of "we don't give a damn." That said, you probably won't either—the food really is that good.

The extensive nightly tasting has no formal menu to speak of, but there are plenty of chatty servers ready to describe each dish, sometimes from over their shoulder by another table.

While the cuisine may seem more studied than sumptuous, it is a pleasure-filled adventure. Highlights include the signature raviolo filled with a gently cooked quail egg and fresh ricotta, swimming in brown butter with shaved black truffle. The excellent "fish fry" consists of a lightly battered and pearly white walleye fillet served with tender fava beans and two fried morsels of blackberry and cheese curds.

Cheesecake is also reinvented with layers of sharp Humboldt Fog, nasturtium purée, and nectarine.

▪ 1466 N. Ashland Ave. (at Le Moyne St.)
🚇 Division
✆ (773) 252-1466 — **WEB:** www.schwarestaurant.com
▪ Dinner Tue – Sat   **PRICE: $$$$**

TOCCO ⅓○

Italian

XX | 🍸 ♿ 🏖️   **MAP:** B4

Are we in Milan or Wicker Park? Tocco brings haute design and fashion to the table with such upscale textural touches as polished resin, faux ostrich skin, and bubblegum-pink accents in this sleek black-and-white space. Don your catwalk best before visiting: a fashion-centric display near a long communal table hints at the chichi theme present throughout.

The décor is cutting-edge, but the menu respects and returns to Italian standbys. Gnocco fritto, a doughy pillow served with charcuterie, is irresistible to even the most willowy fashionistas; while cracker-crisp artisan pizzas from wood-burning ovens are equally pleasing. Traditional involtini di pollo, pounded thin and rolled around prosciutto, gets a hit of brightness from lemon and white wine sauce.

▦ 1266 N. Milwaukee Ave. (bet. Ashland Ave. & Paulina St.)
🚇 Division
📞 (773) 687-8895 — **WEB:** www.toccochicago.com
▦ Dinner Tue – Sun   **PRICE:** $$

TRENCH ⅓○

American

XX | 🍸 🖨️   **MAP:** A3

Sporting a recent menu revamp, the restaurant formerly known as Trenchermen has morphed into Trench. Equal parts watering hole and restaurant, the current iteration offers quirky American cuisine grounded in comfort and seasonality. Given the ample size of the bar, it's easy to assume drinks take precedence here, but the quality ingredients and ambitious cooking merit their own spotlight.

Everything on the menu is tasty in its own right, but it's the perfectly al dente agnolotti that really steals the show. Filled with English pea and ricotta and then glazed with a reduced chicken brodo topped with spring peas, tender morels, and slivers of crisp asparagus, it's heaven on a plate—complete with a tuft of aerated parmigiano on top for an ethereal finish.

▦ 2039 W. North Ave. (bet. Hoyne & Milwaukee Aves.)
🚇 Damen (Blue)
📞 (773) 661-1540 — **WEB:** www.trenchbar.com
▦ Lunch Sat – Sun   Dinner nightly   **PRICE:** $$$

TWO 😊

American

✗✗ | 🍸 🍺 ♿   **MAP:** C5

Two is an urban interpretation of a Midwest tavern that was set up by two owners, features second-hand furnishings, and has an address whose last digit is—you guessed it—the number two. Beyond the vintage Toledo scales, find a reclaimed wood-paneled space dressed with antique meat cleavers, quaint ceiling fans, and large barn doors.

This is a perfect lead into the farm-to-fork cuisine being whipped up in the open kitchen (the banquette across from it affords the best view). Start with classic Southern pimento cheese served in a miniature Mason jar alongside freshly grilled bread. Elegant small plates include pan-seared and spice-dusted halibut with fava beans and oyster mushrooms. On the sweet front, homemade puppy chow is chilled, crisp, and delicious.

▦ 1132 W. Grand Ave. (at May St.)
🚇 Chicago (Blue)
✆ (312) 624-8363 — **WEB:** www.113two.com
▦ Dinner Tue – Sun   **PRICE: $$**

Share the journey with us!
@MichelinGuideCH
📷 @MichelinInspectors

CHINATOWN & SOUTH

For years, the Red Line was the only true link between Chinatown and the South Loop. They may be neighbors geographically, but continue to remain distinct opposites in the culinary, architectural, and demographic spheres. Recent development on both sides of the line has brought the two worlds closer together, combining old and new flavors that make them irresistible to Chicago food lovers. The Great Chicago Fire spared many of the South Loop's buildings, making this architecture some of the oldest in the city. Residential palaces like the Glessner House and Clark House are now open for tours, but a quick walk along Prairie Avenue gives a self-guided view of marvelous mansions. Further north, those massive former lofts along Printers Row have been converted into condos, hotels, bookstores, and restaurants, as has the landmark Dearborn Station—the oldest train depot in Chicago.

SUN-UP TO SUNDOWN

The South Loop has the breakfast scene covered—quite literally—with dishes piled-high at casual neighborhood spots. Sop up a "South of the Border Benny" adorned with chorizo, or any number of egg favorites including frittata and French toast at **Yolk**, located on the southern end of Grant Park. The aptly named **Chicago Waffles** smothers

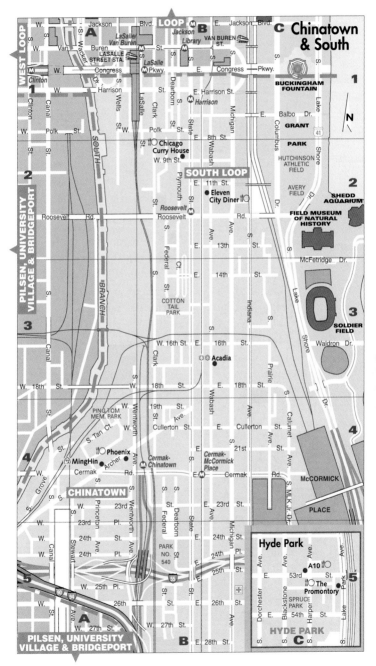

W. Jackson Blvd.

E. Jackson Blvd.

Chinatown & South

LaSalle/ Van Buren

Jackson Library

Van Buren St.

Van Buren St.

S. Wacker

LASALLE STREET STA.

LaSalle St.

W. Congress Pkwy.

LaSalle Pkwy.

E. Congress Pkwy.

BUCKINGHAM FOUNTAIN

WEST LOOP

Clinton

W. Harrison St.

E. Harrison St.

N

1

Clinton

Canal

Wells St.

LaSalle St.

Clark St.

Harrison

Harrison St.

Dearborn St.

State St.

Michigan

Balbo Dr.

Lake Shore

41

W. Polk St.

S. Polk St.

8th St.

Columbus

GRANT

Chicago Curry House

Wabash

PARK

HUTCHINSON ATHLETIC FIELD

W. 9th St.

SOUTH

BRANCH

PILSEN, UNIVERSITY VILLAGE & BRIDGEPORT

2

Polk St.

Plymouth

11th St.

South Loop

AVERY FIELD

SHEDD AQUARIUM

Eleven City Diner

Roosevelt

Roosevelt

Ave.

Rd.

FIELD MUSEUM OF NATURAL HISTORY

Canal

St.

Roosevelt Rd.

Federal St.

E. 13th St.

Lake Shore Dr.

McFetridge Dr.

E. 14th St.

Ct.

St.

COTTON TAIL PARK

3

Clark

Indiana

SOLDIER FIELD

W. 16th St.

E. 16th St.

St.

Waldron Dr.

Acadia

Prairie Ave.

W. 18th

W. 18th St.

E. 18th St.

PING TOM MEM. PARK

Wentworth

W. 19th St.

Wabash Ave.

Calumet Ave.

4

S. Tan Ct.

W. Cullerton St.

Cullerton St.

Phoenix

Archer Ave.

E. 21st St.

MingHin

Cermak- Chinatown

Cermak Rd.

E. Cermak Rd.

McCORMICK

S. MLK Jr. Dr.

Grove

Cermak Rd.

CHINATOWN

E. 23rd St.

PLACE

W. 23rd Pl.

Princeton

Wentworth

23rd St.

Dearborn

State Ave.

E. 24th St.

Hyde Park

W. 24th St.

Canal

Stewart

24th Pl.

Federal St.

PARK NO. 540

E. 24th Pl.

E. 25th St.

Dorchester Ave.

Blackstone Ave.

A10

53rd St.

Harper Ave.

Lake Park Ave.

5

90 94

W. 25th Pl.

55

26th St.

E. 26th St.

The Promontory

SPRUCE PARK

E. 54th

W. 27th St.

E. 27th St.

HYDE PARK

its signature squares with both sweet and savory flavors. Varieties like cheddar cheese are topped with coffee-braised short ribs, while red velvet waffles come with strawberry compote and whipped cream cheese. As long as you're adding to your cholesterol count, stop at one of the many locations of **Ricobene's** for a breaded steak sandwich or a big slab of juicy barbecue ribs.

If you're strolling through the Museum Campus for lunch, grab cash for a bite at **Kim & Carlo's Hot Dog Stand** between the Field Museum and Shedd Aquarium. Vegetarians applaud their special veggie dog with all the Chicago toppings, while everyone gets a great skyline view from Grant Park. For a glimpse of real Windy City politics in action, grab a seat at **Manny's**, the venerable coffee shop and deli. Then sink your teeth into a giant pastrami on rye or a plate of crispy potato pancakes, while watching the city's wheelers and dealers do business.

When night falls, the South Loop really gets rocking. Buddy Guy himself often hits the stage at **Buddy Guy's Legends**, where live blues ring out nightly. Catch a set while digging into classic Southern soul food like fried okra, gumbo, or jambalaya. Similarly **The Velvet Lounge**, founded by late jazz legend Fred Anderson, moved from

the local population is still predominantly Chinese-American and history happily co-exists with contemporary life. The two-story outdoor **Chinatown Square** mall encompasses everything from restaurants and small boutiques to big banks, thereby giving the community a buzzing culinary and cultural introduction. Many of the restaurants here offer classic Chinese-American fare that is an amalgam of Sichuan and Cantonese cuisines, but for a homemade spread stock up on all things authentic from **Chinatown Market**. This large and yet crowded "super" store is outfitted with endless rows of Lee Kum Kee sauces, seafood, fresh produce, and more. At local standby **Go 4 Food**, a Sichuan beef lunch combo or wok-fried and hundred-spiced chicken continue to sate those pungent palates. Let the kids pick out a few intriguing Japanese sweets at **Aji Ichiban**, housed in the Chinatown Square mall, where bins filled with rainbows of foil-wrapped Japanese candy offer opportunities for tricks or treats. Unless

its original location in 2006, but still puts on a heckuva show. Other cutting edge and contemporary musicians also perform here several times a week. For a blast from the past but of a different sort, comedy and history come together at **Tommy Gun's Garage**. This dolled-up speakeasy hosts a riotous dinner theater that also allows the audience to participate.

CHINATOWN

That ornate and arched gate at Wentworth Avenue and Cermak Road welcomes locals and visitors alike to one of the largest Chinatowns in America. This iconic structure is an apt symbol for the neighborhood, where

you can read the characters on the wrappers, you're in for a surprise—though the store offers samples before charging by the pound. Home cooks as well as haute chefs know Chinatown isn't just a destination for dining out. It's also great for filling up on all the good eats necessary for a great home-cooked meal. In fact, the entire neighborhood is a specialty marketplace of sorts: find a mind-boggling array of fresh-pulled noodles at **Mayflower Food**; while Hong Kong-based tea shop, **Saint's Alp Teahouse**, serves quick snacks and a variety of tea-based drinks including the widely popular milk tea and taro milk tea—with or without tapioca pearls. Freshly baked fortune and almond cookies are a revelation at **Golden Dragon Fortune Cookies**, but those craving a wider range of sweets may pour over the cases at **Chiu Quon Bakery** filled with cakes and other cream- or custard-filled pastries. Meanwhile, additional inspiration can be found by perusing a cookbook or two from the Chinatown branch of Chicago's Public Library. Finally, pay homage to the perennial city pastime by watching the White Sox do their thing on Guaranteed Rate Field, or the "Monsters of the Midway" take the gridiron inside Soldier Field's formidable walls.

Museums and learning centers showcase the Windy City's heritage from all angles. Apart from the stately collection of historic buildings in Grant Park's Museum Campus, this neighborhood is also home to Willie Dixon's Blues Heaven Foundation, whose mission is to preserve its musical legacy. With swooping green roof ornaments, the Harold Washington Library Center is impossible to miss, but an equally worthy site is the glass-ceilinged winter garden hidden inside. **Iron Street Farm**, a seven-acre urban field in Bridgeport, is part of Chicago's focus on eradicating food deserts within city limits. Here, local residents grow vegetables, raise chickens, and cultivate bees as part of the farm's educational programs. Respect!

ACADIA ✿ ✿

Contemporary

XxX | 🍸 ♿ 🖨 🍽

Set between glassy apartment buildings and a popular dog park, Acadia is a distinct stand-alone destination. The unexpected yet elegant space employs nothing but neutral grays that extend from the concrete façade to the cushioned chairs and silvery beads dividing the center of this lofty room in half. Service is gracious and professional—the kind we should all expect but is hard to find.

Chef Ryan McCaskey infuses his precise and highly technical cooking with subtle personal touches. Time spent in Maine and his Vietnamese heritage often inform the ambitious tasting menus on offer. The kitchen's commitment is palpable with every course.

Dishes can be both fun and soigné, as in the cheeky take on a "Filet-o-Fish" sandwich, served here as flaky Icelandic cod in crisp golden pan de mie with sauce gribiche and a dab of brandade. Burrata is an inherently perfect food, but is further elevated here with a cool, intense cocoa-prune consommé and mastic foam. Dessert courses bring grand finales such as a neat mound of sweetened butternut squash purée with cranberry gelée, toasted marshmallow cream, and a thin ribbon of pulled caramel. Elaborate mignardises are a fitting end to such a meal.

▪ 1639 S. Wabash Ave. (bet. 16th & 18th Sts.)
🚇 Cermak-Chinatown
✆ (312) 360-9500 — **WEB:** www.acadiachicago.com
▪ Dinner Wed – Sun   **PRICE: $$$$**

A10 ℱ○

Italian

XX | ♿   **MAP:** C5

A10 is a highway that winds through the Italian Riviera, but its detour through Hyde Park comes courtesy of prolific restaurateur, Matthias Merges. University of Chicago students and staff populate this split space, building a buzz over marble-topped rounds in the low-key bar area or dark wood tables in the convivial dining room.

Elegant presentations and ambitious creativity set this kitchen apart. Dishes deftly balance the rustic and sophisticated at a fantastic value, as in the pretty composition of charred and lightly blanched carrots over ricotta that is tinged pink from beet juice. Grilled salmon is beautifully cooked, flaky yet crisp-skinned, and served alongside creamy potato confit and large chunks of pickled cauliflower and carrots.

▪ 1462 E. 53rd St. (at Harper Ave.)
℘ (773) 288-1010 — **WEB:** www.a10hydepark.com
▪ Dinner Tue – Sun   **PRICE:** $$

CHICAGO CURRY HOUSE ℱ○

Indian

XX | ♿ 🍽   **MAP:** B2

Maybe you sniff the wafting aromas of ginger, garlic, and cumin first; maybe you hear the sitar tinkling its welcoming notes as you enter. Either way, you know immediately that Chicago Curry House is a commendable showcase of Indian and Nepalese cuisines.

The lunchtime buffet lets you eat your fill for under $12, with crispy papadum and baskets of naan; while dinner features an à la carte of faves including Nepalese khasi ko maasu with bone-in goat bobbing in a velvety cardamom- and black pepper-sauce. Tandoori chicken is a smoky, moist delight; and butter chicken, creamy and rich in a tomato- and garam masala-spiced gravy, is done just right. The staff has helpful suggestions for dealing with the area's draconian parking restrictions; call ahead for tips.

▪ 899 S. Plymouth Ct. (at 9th St.)
🚇 Harrison
℘ (312) 362-9999 — **WEB:** www.curryhouseonline.com
▪ Lunch & dinner daily   **PRICE:** ☜☜

ELEVEN CITY DINER 🍴○

Deli

🍴 | ♿ 🪑 ⬜ 🧳

MAP: B2

Nosh on a mile-high sandwich or chocolate malt at Eleven City Diner, a modern revival of the classic Jewish deli. Gleaming subway tiles play off retro leather booths and swiveling barstools, while jazz in the background keeps things moving with chutzpah and finesse.

Diner standards include patty melts, sandwiches piled with corned beef or pastrami, knishes, and latkes. Bubbie's chicken soup comes brimming with a fluffy matzo ball the size of a baseball; while Junior's cheesecake from Brooklyn or a triple-decker wedge of red velvet cake sates all the sweet-loving guests. A full-service deli counter offers salamis and smoked fish to-go. For a true blast from the past, stop by the candy stand near the entry, stocked with Bazooka Joe and other favorites.

▨ 1112 S. Wabash Ave. (bet. 11th St. & Roosevelt Rd.)
🚇 Roosevelt
✆ (312) 212-1112 — **WEB:** www.elevencitydiner.com
▨ Lunch & dinner daily   PRICE: 🪙

MINGHIN 🙂

Chinese

🍴🍴 | ♿ ⬜ 🧳 🥢

MAP: A4

Conveniently situated on the ground level of Chinatown Square, MingHin is a stylish standby that draws a diverse crowd to the neighborhood. Spacious dining rooms separated by wooden lattice panels offer seating for a number of occasions, from casual booths and large banquet-style rounds to specially outfitted tables for hot pots.

Dim sum is a popular choice even on weekdays, with diners making selections from photographic menus rather than waiting for a passing cart. Among the numerous options, juicy har gao, stuffed with plump seasoned shrimp, always hits the spot. Pan-fried turnip cakes are simultaneously crispy and creamy, studded with bits of pork and mushroom. Fluffy and subtly sweet Malay steamed egg cake is a rare find for dessert.

▨ 2168 S. Archer Ave. (at Princeton Ave.)
🚇 Cermak-Chinatown
✆ (312) 808-1999 — **WEB:** www.minghincuisine.com
▨ Lunch & dinner daily   PRICE: $$

PHOENIX 🍴

Chinese

✕✕ | ♿ 🖥 🚿 🥢   **MAP:** A4

Dim sum lovers get the best of both worlds at Phoenix, a comfortable room that boasts a grand view of the Chicago skyline. Here, stacks of bamboo baskets are wheeled to tables on signature silver trolleys for a classic dim sum experience—yet each diner's selection is cooked to order for truly fresh and steaming hot bites. The proof is in the soft and poppable shrimp-and-chive dumplings and the fluffy white buns stuffed with chunks of barbecue pork.

Those looking for larger portions will appreciate the meandering menu, which also boasts Hong Kong-style stir-fry and clay pot dishes alongside Americanized Chinese classics. Fillets of steamed sea bass swim in soy oil on a large oval platter, sprinkled with a touch of slivered scallion to brighten the delicately flaky fish.

🔲 2131 S. Archer Ave. (bet. Princeton & Wentworth Aves.)
🔳 Cermak-Chinatown
📞 (312) 328-0848 — **WEB:** www.chinatownphoenix.com
🔲 Lunch & dinner daily   **PRICE:** 🍜

THE PROMONTORY 🍴

American

✕✕ | 🍸 🏠 🖥 🧊   **MAP:** C5

Equal parts restaurant, watering hole, and music venue, The Promontory brings a much-needed gathering place to the Hyde Park community. Under lofty ceilings trimmed with black iron beams and sleek wood accents, urbanites sip hand-crafted cocktails around a central bar.

A white-hot fire blazes away in the open kitchen, providing the "hearth to table" food trumpeted on the menu. Smoky roasted feta arrives in a pool of balsamic vinegar and oil with a generous assortment of briny olives, while shatteringly crisp black trumpet mushrooms and pickled shallot add piquant crunch to Nantucket bay scallops. At dessert, sweet brûléed marshmallow and a scoop of graham cracker ice cream sit atop a moist chocolate soufflé for a reverse take on s'mores.

🔲 5311 S. Lake Park Ave. West (bet. 53rd & 54th Sts.)
📞 (312) 801-2100 — **WEB:** www.promontorychicago.com
🔲 Lunch & dinner daily   **PRICE:** $$

GOLD COAST

GLITZ & GLAMOUR

The moniker says it all: the Gold Coast is one of the Windy City's poshest neighborhoods, flaunting everything from swanky high-rises along Lake Shore Drive to dazzling boutiques dotting Michigan Avenue. Stroll down the Magnificent Mile only to discover that money can indeed buy it all. Then, head over to Oak Street for yet another spree and watch millionaires mingle over Manolos while heiresses rummage for handbags.

APPLAUDING THE ARTS

Through all this allure, Gold Coast architecture is not just notable but stunning. And, mansions crafted in regal Queen Anne, Georgian Revival, or Richardsonian Romanesque styles are unequivocally breathtaking. However, this neighborhood is not all about the glitz; it is also deeply committed to the arts as a whole, housing both the Museum of Contemporary Art and the world-leading Newberry Library. Culture vultures are sure to uncover something edgy and unique at A Red Orchid Theater, after which the exotic Indian lunchtime buffet at **Gaylord** seems not only opportune, but perhaps obligatory? This prized subterranean location, with its spelled-out menu items and well-stocked bar, is sought by both aficionados as well as anyone hungering for free appetizers during happy hour. Nearby, **Le Cordon Bleu College of Culinary Arts** continues to train students (read: hot chefs in the making) on the classics, as well as the next food fad in Chicago's kitchens.

RAUCOUS NIGHTS

It's a well-known fact that the Gold Coast also knows how to party. Visit any nightclub, pub, or restaurant along Rush and Division to get a sense of how the cool kids hold it down—until well after dawn. By then,

find breakfast on the burner at **The Original Pancake House**. This may seem like a lowbrow treat for such a high-brow neighborhood, but really can there be anything more rewarding than fluffy pancakes, towering waffles, and sizzling skillet eggs after a late night?

There is also some darn good junk food to be had in this white-gloved capital of prosperity. American comfort classics like sliders, burgers, and mac and cheese find their way into the menu at **LuxBar**, a dynamic lounge-cum-bar that proffers some of the best people-watching in town. Need some sweet?

Make your way to one of **Teuscher's** outposts for decadent dark chocolate or even **Corner Bakery Cafe** for a fleet of bakery fresh treats—the golden-brown cinnamon crème cake topped with crumbles of cinnamon streusel and powdered sugar has been drawing residents for over two decades now and is (rightfully) dubbed a signature.

A QUICK FIX

With so many awards under its belt and boasting the best ingredients in town, **Gold Coast Dogs** is packed to the gills (er, buns), perpetually. Inside, everyone is either a regular or on the verge of becoming one—thanks in large part to their deliciously charred dogs, usually topped with gooey cheddar. Or, simply humor your hot dog hankering by joining the constant queue outside **Downtown Dogs**. Surely these robust eats should be sealed by a cup that revives? **TeaGschwendner** is just the spot where locals have been known to lose themselves in a world of exotic selections. And, if you don't feel like steeping your own "Sencha Claus" blend, then snag a seat at **Argo Tea** where clouds of whipped cream and flavorful iced drinks are all part of the carte—it's just like Starbucks without the coffee! Serious cooks and gourmands make a beeline for **The Spice House**, where a spectrum of high quality and often esoteric spices, seasonings, and rubs (ground and blended in-house) make for an integral part of a dinner party at home.

HEAVEN ON EARTH

In keeping with its quintessentially elegant and old-world repute, the Gold Coast allows you to don Grandma's pearls for afternoon tea at **The Drake's Palm Court**. Daintily sip, not slurp, your tea while listening to the gentle strumming of a harp and sampling a divine selection of finger sandwiches, flaky pastries, and buttery scones. If it's good enough for the Queen, it will certainly do. Also housed in The Drake, warm and luxurious **Coq d'Or ape** is famous for its classic cocktails, comfort food specials, and live weekend entertainment. And finally, over on Delaware Place, fine wines plus cocktails aren't the only thing heating up the scene at **Drumbar**—a rooftop spot at the Raffaello Hotel that lets the fashionable crowd frolic alfresco at night (and during the day on Sunday).

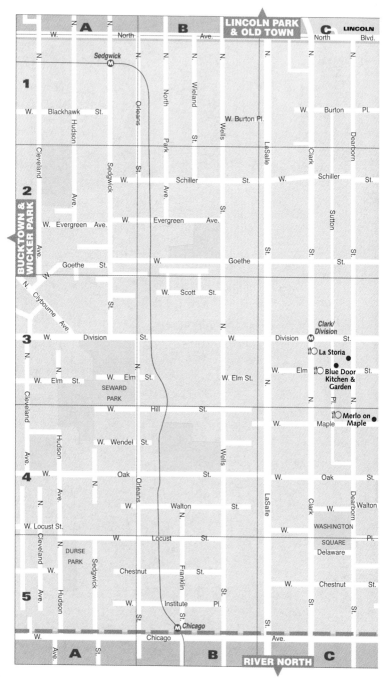

W.   North   Ave.   North   Blvd.

Sedgwick M

1

W.   Blackhawk   St.

N. Hudson

N. Cleveland Ave.

N. Sedgwick Ave.

N. Orleans St.

N. Park St.

N. Wieland St.

N. North Ave.

N. Wells St.

W. Burton Pl.

W.   Burton   Pl.

N. LaSalle St.

N. Clark St.

N. Dearborn St.

2

W.   Schiller   St.

W.   Schiller   St.

W.   Evergreen   Ave.

W.   Evergreen   Ave.

N. Sutton St.

N. Clybourne Ave.

Goethe   St.

W.   Goethe   St.

W.   Scott   St.

3

W.   Division   St.

W.   Division   St.

Clark/Division M

⭐️○ La Storia

W.   Elm   St.

W.   Elm   St.

W. Elm St.

W.   Elm   St.

⭐️○ Blue Door Kitchen & Garden

SEWARD PARK

W.   Hill   St.

W.   Maple

⭐️○ Merlo on Maple

W.   Wendel   St.

N. Cleveland Ave.

N. Hudson Ave.

N. Orleans St.

N. Wells St.

4

W.   Oak   St.

W.   Oak   St.

W.   Walton   St.

W.   Walton   St.

N. LaSalle St.

N. Clark St.

N. Dearborn St.

WASHINGTON

W. Locust St.

W.   Locust   St.

SQUARE

DURSE PARK

Delaware

5

N. Cleveland Ave.

N. Hudson Ave.

N. Sedgwick St.

W.   Chestnut   St.

N. Franklin St.

W.   Chestnut   St.

W.   Institute   Pl.

N. Wells St.

Chicago M

W.   Chicago   Ave.

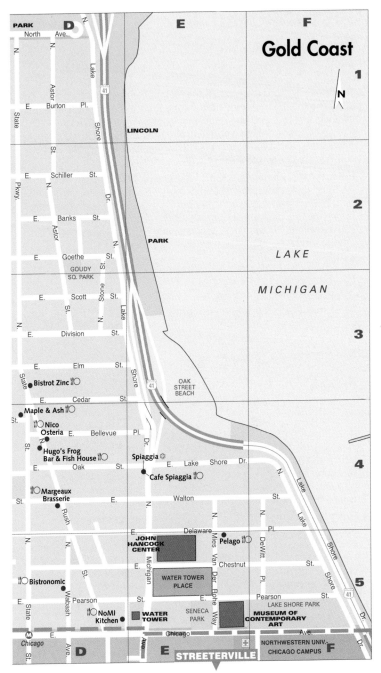

Gold Coast

N

LAKE MICHIGAN

OAK
STREET
BEACH

Bistrot Zinc ‖○

Maple & Ash ‖○

‖○ Nico
Osteria

Hugo's Frog
Bar & Fish House ‖○

Spiaggia ✳

Cafe Spiaggia ‖○

‖○ Margeaux
Brasserie

Pelago ‖○

JOHN
HANCOCK
CENTER

‖○ Bistronomic

WATER TOWER
PLACE

Pearson

LAKE SHORE PARK

‖○ NoMI
Kitchen

WATER
TOWER

SENECA
PARK

MUSEUM OF
CONTEMPORARY
ART

Chicago

STREETERVILLE

NORTHWESTERN UNIV.-
CHICAGO CAMPUS

BISTRONOMIC ¶O

French

XX | ♿ 🏠 🖥 🍸 🖐

Tucked away from the buzz of the Magnificent Mile, Bistronomic is a great place to cool your tired heels. Jaunty red awnings beckon brightly, and the revolving door spins guests into a warm room that's focused on the bonhomie of dining with friends. Oxblood walls, gray banquettes, and a central bar play up the bistro feel, while the kitchen conveys creativity with fresh renditions of tasty classics.

Rusticity and elegance come together in a fillet of Lake Superior whitefish that is pan-seared to golden-brown and matched with spring ratatouille, preserved lemon, and puréed eggplant. Exquisitely crisp feuilletine is a glamorous upgrade to the classic Kit Kat bar, folded with hazelnuts, bittersweet chocolate, and finished with a sweet-tart orange sauce.

▪ 840 N. Wabash Ave. (bet. Chestnut & Pearson Sts.)
▪ Chicago (Red)
✆ (312) 944-8400 — **WEB:** www.bistronomic.net
▪ Lunch Wed – Sun Dinner nightly

PRICE: $$

BISTROT ZINC ¶O

French

XX | ♿ 🍸

If you couldn't tell from the bright red exterior and hand-painted windows, Bistrot Zinc is indeed a classic dressed in mosaic-tiled floors, lemon-tinted walls hung with mirrors, woven rattan chairs, and yes, that curvaceous zinc bar. Suits, locals, and Gold Coast power shoppers populate the tables from lunch through dinner, as white-aproned waiters happily uncork bottles of rouge et blanc.

Don't look for modern surprises on the menu; contentment here is attained through uncomplicated but expertly prepared French dishes from frites to frisée. Whole trout, pan-fried until golden and napped with butter sauce, hits all the right notes; while daily standards like croque monsieur or French onion soup are enhanced by more ambitious monthly specials.

▪ 1131 N. State St. (bet. Elm & Cedar Sts.)
▪ Clark/Division
✆ (312) 337-1131 — **WEB:** www.bistrotzinc.com
▪ Lunch & dinner daily

PRICE: $$

BLUE DOOR KITCHEN & GARDEN 🍴

American

XX | 🏠 🖼 🛶   **MAP:** C3

Thank chef-to-the-stars Art Smith for raising the stakes of the local dining scene with this relaxed bistro, which replaces his former success, Table 52.

In 1871, this carriage house home is said to have survived the Great Chicago Fire. Today, the cozy and well-appointed dining room makes the most of its parquet floors, Louis XV-style chairs, welcoming bar, and open kitchen where Southern-leaning fare is prepared in full view.

The cooking showcases produce from The Farm, located just an hour south of the city, so seasonal dishes like tomato and watermelon salad over greens will be particularly refreshing. Signature desserts, like the towering slice of Hummingbird cake layered with banana and pineapple, are enough to feed two (if not four) diners.

▦ 52 W. Elm St. (bet. Clark & Dearborn Sts.)
🚇 Clark/Division
📞 (312) 573-4000 — **WEB:** www.bluedoorkitchenchicago.com
▦ Lunch & dinner daily   **PRICE:** $$

CAFE SPIAGGIA 🍴

Italian

XX | 🐝 ♿   **MAP:** E4

The revamped look at this café is fresh, modern, and stunning and yet it retains its rustic soul. The clean and sophisticated combination of white marble tables with black cushioned chairs complement the oversized windows' lake views. Gold accents add a sense of luxury and aesthetic appeal to the space, not unlike its über-elegant sibling Spiaggia down the hall.

Like the singular décor, the menu also presents something unique. It is offered as a series of vegetable-focused small plates as well as a handful of larger entrées for two, like the deeply satisfying hunk of pork shoulder, honey-roasted slowly and carefully until it nearly falls off the bone. Standout pasta includes gemelli coated in a tomato sauce studded with cubed guanciale, coppa, and brined artichokes.

▦ 980 N. Michigan Ave. (at Oak St.)
🚇 Chicago (Red)
📞 (312) 280-2750 — **WEB:** www.spiaggiarestaurant.com/cafe
▦ Lunch Mon – Sat   Dinner nightly   **PRICE:** $$

HUGO'S FROG BAR & FISH HOUSE 🍴

American

XX | 🚻 🏠 🖼️   **MAP:** D4

Housed in a sprawling setting adjacent to big brother Gibson's, Hugo's always seems packed. The vast dining room sets white linen-topped tables amid dark polished wood and pale walls decorated with a mounted swordfish, fish prints, and model ships. Hugo's bar draws its own crowds with abundant counter seating.

The menu focuses on a selection of fish preparations as well as steaks and chops. These are supplemented by stone crab claws, oysters, crab cakes, chowders, and sautéed frog's legs. Speaking of which, the restaurant takes its name from the nickname of owner Hugo Ralli's grandfather, General Bruce Hay of Her Majesty's Imperial Forces.

Bring a football team to share a slice of the Muddy Bottom Pie, a decadent (and enormous) ice cream cake.

■ 1024 N. Rush St. (bet. Bellevue Pl. & Oak St.)
🚇 Clark/Division
✆ (312) 640-0999 — **WEB:** www.hugosfrogbar.com
■ Lunch Sat – Sun   Dinner nightly   **PRICE:** $$

LA STORIA 🍴

Italian

XX | 🏠 🖼️ 🛋️ 🍷   **MAP:** C3

Tucked into a gorgeous townhouse along Chicago's Gold Coast, this Italian charmer woos with pretty patios, sexy dark panel walls, and conversation-worthy murals by Edward Sorel. The result is a casual, clubby feel; and the first floor, with its low wood beam ceilings, offers great views of Dearborn Street.

Chef Rey Villalobos, who oversees the rest of Ideology's portfolio of restaurants (including Biggs, Blue Door Farm Stand and Chicago Q), takes the reins here, pushing out a finely executed Italian menu. Try the notable pollo Milanese. While it may seems like a predictable standard, La Storia's version is laid over excellent liver mousse and strewn with crispy fried capers as well as peppery watercress to give it a solid leg up on the competition.

■ 1154 N. Dearborn St. (bet. Division & Elm Sts.)
🚇 Clark/Division
✆ (312) 915-5950 — **WEB:** www.lastoriachicago.com
■ Lunch Sat – Sun   Dinner nightly   **PRICE:** $$$

MAPLE & ASH 🍴

Steakhouse

XXX | 🍸 ♿ 🏠 📷 🧳 🧺   **MAP:** D4

Every meal here is like a party, especially if you arrive with an above-average appetite. The space feels as dynamic as the locale, with an enormous dining room and open kitchen. The menu offers different formats, but the one that seems to be earning attention is the "I Don't Give A (ahem)" prix-fixe, for a premium price. In keeping with the steakhouse theme, portions are gargantuan. Even a wedge salad is a veritable meal of crisped bacon and marinated cherry tomatoes piled over iceberg, draped with blue cheese dressing. The Siberian caviar is as good as its copious sides, from potato chips to cornichons. Steaks are thick, juicy and just right.

At brunch or on the late night, head downstairs to elegant Eightbar, which sports a playful vibe and outdoor seats.

🔲 8 W. Maple St. (bet. Dearborn & State Sts.)
🔲 Clark/Division
📞 (312) 944-8888 — **WEB:** www.mapleandash.com
🔲 Lunch Sun   Dinner nightly   **PRICE:** $$$$

MARGEAUX BRASSERIE 🍴

French

XXX | 🐌 ♿ 📷 🧳 🧺   **MAP:** D4

Margeaux Brasserie is one swank spot. Tucked into the Waldorf Astoria, this restaurant marks the first Chicago venture for the popular Mina Group, led by Michelin-starred Chef Michael Mina. The space is bright and airy, with light streaming in through the large picture windows and lots of luxe velvet and leather details.

Kick things off with a tangy, perfectly caramelized starter of duck wings a' l'orange, before moving on to dishes like warm tomato Tatin, paired with crisp puff pastry, Camembert, shallots and pistou. Then, a luscious bone-in rack of lamb takes satisfaction to the next level with stewed chickpeas, potatoes, piquillo peppers, fennel, turnip with roasted lamb jus, as well as a cigar-shaped croustillant filled with braised lamb rib.

🔲 11 E. Walton St. (at Rush St.)
🔲 Chicago (Red)
📞 (312) 625-1324 — **WEB:** www.michaelmina.net
🔲 Lunch Sat – Sun   Dinner nightly   **PRICE:** $$$

MERLO ON MAPLE 🍴

Italian

XX | 🎴 🖼 📱

MAP: C4

Inside a graciously decorated Victorian townhouse, Chef/owner Luisa Silvia proudly showcases the bounty of her native Bologna with an Emiliano accent and delicious Northern Italian fare. Her frequently changing roster of luscious dishes serve as edible billboards for the celebrated foods of the region—think mortadella di Bologna and tartufi neri dell'Umbria.

Rabbit ragù clings to delicate parsley-flecked bow-tie pasta tossed with Parmigiano Reggiano and copious butter. Wine-braised bone-in lamb shank, served in its own rich sauce, needs little else to shine. Signature budino di mascarpone, cioccolato e caffè is the standard-bearer for proper tiramisù, accompanied by explosively tart sugar-coated red currants to offset the creamy sweetness.

■ 16 W. Maple St. (bet. Dearborn & State Sts.)
■ Clark/Division
✆ (312) 335-8200 — **WEB:** www.merlochicago.com
■ Dinner nightly

PRICE: $$$

NICO OSTERIA 🍴

Italian

XX | ♿ 🌳 🖼 🚗 📋 📱

MAP: D4

Buzzworthy and a hit since day one, Chef Paul Kahan's area darling happens to be one of the most likeable restaurants around. Think of it as more trendsetting than trendy. The dining room enhances the Mediterranean ambience with subway-tile floors and plenty of natural light. The accommodating staff ensures that no one leaves disappointed.

The menu focuses on Italian-leaning seafood dishes, so it is an ideal stop for inspired crudo like fluke with ice-wine vinegar, fennel, and breadcrumbs. Take a counter seat before the open kitchen to see just how the Kindai tuna with black trumpet mushrooms and kumquat comes together. The regional menu may go on to highlight dishes with boldy flavored seafood, like chili-cured swordfish with thin, house-made grissini.

■ 1015 Rush St. (at Oak St.)
■ Chicago (Brown)
✆ (312) 994-7100 — **WEB:** www.nicoosteria.com
■ Lunch & dinner daily

PRICE: $$$

NOMI KITCHEN ¡○

American

XxX | 💥 🍷 ♿ 🏠 🖥 🗄 🛏 👖   **MAP:** D5

A hushed aerie awaits on the seventh floor of the Park Hyatt at NoMI Kitchen. Let the dapper staff whisk you through the hotel lobby and elevator to a glassed-in dining room with Water Tower views. A semi-open kitchen led by Executive Chef Edward Sura doesn't detract from the lush but restrained décor, and a breezy terrace offers an alfresco option with a different menu.

The kitchen's impressive and ingredient-driven dishes are equally inspired by Eastern and Western cuisines. Fish makes for a seaworthy selection of sushi and maki, while pickled pepper jam and pine nut streusel pair with orbs of fried caponata-style eggplant that are both crispy on the outside and silky within. End with a parade of house-made ice cream flavors like toasted vanilla marshmallow.

🔲 800 N. Michigan Ave. (entrance on Chicago Ave.)
🔲 Chicago (Red)
✆ (312) 239-4030 — **WEB:** www.nomirestaurant.com
🔲 Lunch & dinner daily   **PRICE: $$$**

PELAGO ¡○

Italian

XxX | ♿ 🏠 🖥 🗄   **MAP:** E5

This jewel box of a spot is fittingly set adjacent to the Raffaello Hotel. Oozing with elegance, it boasts a crisp style via large windows, tasteful artwork, and comfortable leather seats. An azure-blue color theme ensures the mood is serene. If the décor doesn't evoke the Med, then the Italian-leaning dishes will do the trick. Taralli ricotta alla salsiccia features ampersand-shaped pockets filled with ricotta and bathed in a white wine sauce enriched by Parmigiano Reggiano for a carbo-licious feast. Guazzetto di cernia e capesante, or grouper and scallops in a subtle tomato broth, is matched with escarole for all that's wholesome in this world.

Some may swap dessert for cheese, but don't forgo the frollino—a cookie ring filled with mango-mascarpone sabayon.

🔲 201 E. Delaware Pl. (at Mies van der Rohe Way)
🔲 Chicago (Red)
✆ (312) 280-0700 — **WEB:** www.pelagorestaurant.com
🔲 Lunch & dinner daily   **PRICE: $$$**

SPIAGGIA 🌸
Italian

XXX | 🍇 🍸 🍺 ♿ ⊡ 🖐

There are many reasons why Spiaggia remains one of Chicago's most beloved Italian restaurants. There are high-end bells and whistles aplenty, but to hear the staff recite the effort and intricacies of, say, the culurgiones is to compel you to order them. These curious "ravioli" of sorts deliver pure pleasure, filled with lamb, fava beans, and shallots, then baked and served over a pool of fava sauce with crisp radishes. Even the bread here is a noteworthy artisanal assortment, including a crusty little pain boule begging to be smeared with butter. Steak is then treated with particular care—in this case the perfectly marbled ribeye, which is dry-aged for 45 days before being cooked to a medium rare and topped with shaved bottarga and "brown cow" parmesan, alongside ramps, oyster mushrooms, and an intriguing espresso-Hollandaise sauce.

Come dessert, the tiramisu has all the flavors and notes of the classic, but is deconstructed with contemporary style.

All in all, to dine at Spiaggia is to celebrate a Chicago grande-dame. The dining room is designed with marble columns and terraces to make the most of its dramatic views—an idyllic spot to appreciate the Magnificent Mile by night.

▨ 980 N. Michigan Ave. (at Oak St.)
🚇 Chicago (Red)
📞 (312) 280-2750 — **WEB:** www.spiaggiarestaurant.com
▨ Dinner nightly

PRICE: $$$$

HUMBOLDT PARK & LOGAN SQUARE

ALBANY PARK · IRVING PARK

A charming pair of lively North Side neighborhoods, Humboldt Park and Logan Square have for long been revered as Chicagoland's heart and soul. They may reside a few steps off the beaten path, but locals here still live to eat and can be found perusing the wares of global grocers, secret bodegas, and those fine falafel shops. **Smalls** is one such tasty smoke hut that churns out familiar barbecue dishes alongside Asian comfort food. Here, hickory-smoked brisket on Texas toast with Thai-style "tiger cry" sauce has earned an army of devotees for good reason. Koreatown is a prized thoroughfare spanning miles along Lawrence Avenue and preparing faithful meals that commence with banchan, followed by galbi, bulgogi, or bibimbap. **Joong Boo Market** is a gem in Avondale flaunting specialties from rice cakes and ground red pepper flakes to dried vegetables and seaweed snacks. Stroll further along these tree-lined streets dotted

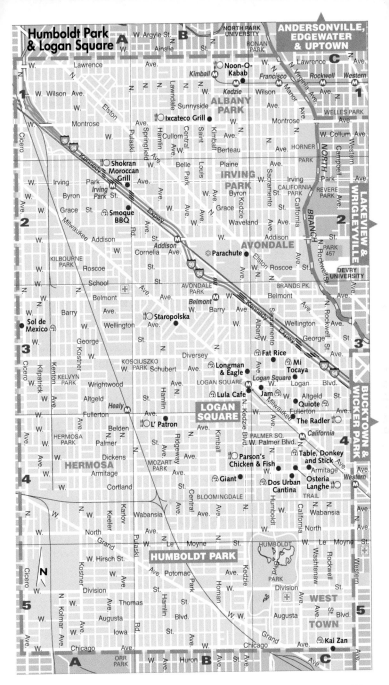

NORTH PARK UNIVERSITY

W. Argyle St.

Ainslie   St.

RONAN PARK

Noon-O-Kabab

Kimball

Lawrence   Ave.

W. Lawrence   Ave.

Rockwell   Western

N. Virginia Ave.

N. Manor   Ave.

Kedzie   Wilson

Francisco

1   W. Wilson Ave.

WELLES PARK

ALBANY PARK

Sunnyside   Ave.

W. Collum   Ave.

Montrose

Ixcateco Grill

HORNER PARK

Cullom   Ave.

Berteau

Belle   Plaine

IRVING PARK

Byron

CALIFORNIA PARK

Irving   Park

REVERE PARK

Shokran Moroccan Grill

Irving Park St.

Grace   St.

Byron

Grace

Waveland

2   Smoque BBQ

Addison

Addison   Ave.

AVONDALE

DEVRY UNIVERSITY

Cornelia   Ave.

Parachute

Roscoe   St.

Roscoe

PARK 457

KILBOURNE PARK

School

AVONDALE PARK

BRANDS PK.

Belmont

Belmont

Sol de Mexico

Barry   Ave.

Belmont

Wellington

Wellington

3   George   St.

Staropolska

Diversey

Fat Rice

Mi Tocaya

KOSCIUSZKO PARK

Schubert   Ave.

Longman & Eagle

Logan   Blvd.

KELVYN PARK

Wrightwood

LOGAN SQUARE

Logan

Altgeld

Jam

Quiote

Lula Cafe

Healy

Fullerton

Fullerton   Ave.

The Radler

4   L' Patron

LOGAN SQUARE

PALMER SQ.

California

HERMOSA PARK

Belden

W. Palmer Blvd.

Palmer

Parson's Chicken & Fish

Table, Donkey and Stick

Dickens

MOZART PARK

Armitage

Osteria Langhe

Giant

Dos Urban Cantina

Armitage

Cortland

BLOOMINGDALE

TRAIL

Wabansia   Ave.

Keeler

Karlov

Humboldt   Ave.

Wabansia

North

North

HUMBOLDT PARK

Le   Moyne   St.

Le Moyne   St.

W. Hirsch St.

HUMBOLDT PARK

Rockwell

Washtenaw

Potomac   St.

Division

Division   Ave.

WEST

5   Division

Thomas

Augusta

TOWN

Augusta   Blvd.

Iowa   St.

Chicago   Ave.

Chicago

Kai Zan

A   ORR PARK   W. Huron   St.   **B**   Ave.   **C**

N

home to a vibrant Puerto Rican community—just look for Paseo Boricua, the flag-shaped steel gateway demarcating the district along Division Street. These storefronts are as much a celebration of the diaspora as the homeland, with an impressive array of traditional foods, rare ingredients, and authentic pernil. In fact, the annual **Puerto Rican Festival** features four days of festivity, fun, and great food. You can also get your fill of Caribbean cuisine in these parts, but for serious Latin food, dash over to **Café Colao**, a Puerto Rican coffee shop also selling pastries and sandwiches. Get here before the crowds for a cheese-and-guava *pastelillo* or Cuban sandwich with *cafe con leche*, of course.

with quaint buildings and trendy shops, until you land upon **Bang Bang Pie Shop**. Here, handmade buttery biscuits are likely to keep you inside—indefinitely. But, make sure to step out and into **Global Garden**, a community venture (or "refugee training farm") where immigrants grow produce for sale at local farmer's markets or CSAs. Other like-minded operations include **Campbell Co-op** or **Drake Garden** whose harvest of vegetables and plants unite the neighborhood's diverse groups, while ensuring gorgeous greenery amid the city. Humboldt Park is also

Bill Dugan's **The Fishguy Market** has been serving Michelin-starred restaurants for decades, while also renting space to **Wellfleet**, a popular luncheonette named after the Cape Cod fishing town. Here fish fans are always in good hands thanks to the kitchen's creative renditions of fresh crustaceans. If steaming hot dogs are a custom in Chicago, then **Jimmy's Red Hots** is the standard bearer of this neighborhood. Meanwhile, the great value found at **Dante's Pizzeria** may only be exceeded by its larger-than-life, exceedingly tasty pies. Speaking of which, the aptly named "inferno" comes with pepperoni, sausage, bacon, and fresh garlic—just in case those blazing hot peppers aren't enough. Alternatively, take a real gamble and go for the slice of the day. Pastries take the cake at **Shokolad** and the staff at this Ukrainian haunt knows how to keep your eyes on the prize: a stacked-to-the-top glass bakery case showcases its wares to great effect. Their signature cheesecake lollipops may not hail from the Old Country, but rest assured that they are very tasty.

LOGAN SQUARE

An eclectic mix of cuisines combined with historic buildings and charming boulevards attracts everybody from hipsters and working-class locals, as well as artists and students to this lovely quarter. Within the culinary community, a blend of home chefs, star cooks, and staunch foodies can be found plunging into the products at **Kurowski's Sausage Shop**, a respected butcher specializing in handmade cuts of Polish meats. Novices take note:

pair a flavorful sausage with toasted rye before picking up pickles to-go from the old-school and always-reliable **Dill Pickle Food Co-op**. Then tuck into neighborhood cafe **Cellar Door Provisions** for a variety of from-scratch baked breads, as well as European-style pastries. Carrying on this cultural explosion, Logan Square is also home to **Johnny's Grill**, a neighborhood diner that has been revived by a formally trained pastry chef. But the greasy spoon spirit lives on in dishes like the fried fish sandwich, flat top double cheeseburger, and bottomless fresh-brewed **Intelligentsia** coffee. Also of epicurean note is **Logan Square Farmers Market** selling everything ingestible from raw honey to organic zucchini; while the uniquely sourced and beautifully packaged brews at **Gaslight Coffee Roasters** are a caffeine junkie's real-life fantasy.

Just as kids delight in a day spent at **Margie's Candies** for homemade chocolates, adults eagerly await a night out at **Scofflaw** for gin-infused libations and secret menu combinations. Of course, the tiki craze is thriving at local cocktail legend Paul McGee's **Lost Lake Tiki Bar**, slinging rum-based delights. On the opposite end, students prepare for an impromptu dinner with nonna by buying up all things authentic from the **Half Italian Grocer**. Food wonks however shop till they drop at **Independence Park Farmers Market** for a divine dinner back home. Less locally traditional but just as tantalizing is **Jimmy's Pizza Café**, rightfully mobbed for its mean rendition of a New York-style slice.

Albany Park is yet another melting pot of global foods and gastronomic retreats minus the sky-high price. Plan your own Middle Eastern feast with a spectrum of cheeses, spreads, and flatbreads from **Al-Khyam Bakery & Grocery**, tailed by perfect baklava from **Nazareth Sweets**. But if meat is what you're craving, then join the crowd of carnivores at **Charcoal Delights**, a time-tested burger joint.

DOS URBAN CANTINA 😃

Mexican

✗✗ | 🍸 🍴 📠   **MAP:** C4

After several years at Topolobampo, the husband-wife duo behind this gem have taken their knowledge and skills to craft this consistently delicious and inventive cuisine. And, the chefs' deep understanding of Mexican ingredients has allowed them to create elegant and well-priced compositions. Chunks of slowly braised pork carnitas are hearty, tender, and brought to an entirely new level with squash that pops with bright flavor—all balanced with a bracing tomatillo broth. For dessert, indulge in excellent Mexican sugar pie topped with whipped cream and pecan toffee that is out of this world.

The space is comfortable and roomy so that the steady stream of thirty-somethings never make it feel crowded. Curved booths and romantic lighting lend a soft feel.

🟦 2829 W. Armitage Ave. (at Mozart St.)
📞 (773) 661-6452 — **WEB:** www.dosurbancantina.com
🟦 Dinner Wed – Sun   **PRICE: $$**

FAT RICE 😃

Macanese

✗✗ | ♿ 📠   **MAP:** C3

Not familiar with the food of Macau? Not to worry—Fat Rice turns the uninitiated into believers nightly. In fact, the restaurant's thriving success led to an expansion that includes a cocktail lounge and bakery next door. Bar seating around the open kitchen gives a bird's-eye view of the mélange of ingredients used in each dish, though servers are happy to walk any guest through the intoxicating mashup of Portuguese-meets-Asian cuisine.

Sharing is recommended for the namesake arroz gordo, a paella-esque blend of meat, shellfish, and pickles. Pillowy bread pairs well with crisp chili prawns stuffed with a flavorful blend of fermented black beans and garlic; while chrysanthemum gelée served with jackfruit and peanuts is a sweet 'n salty thrill.

🟦 2957 W. Diversey Ave. (at Sacramento Ave.)
🚇 Logan Square
📞 (773) 661-9170 — **WEB:** www.eatfatrice.com
🟦 Lunch Wed – Sun   Dinner Tue – Sat   **PRICE: $$**

GIANT ☺

American

✗   **MAP:** B4

Brought to you by Jason Vincent, this fabulous and friendly restaurant is an epitome of the Windy City. The menu is a listing of familiar dishes (think onion rings, crab salad, and baby back ribs), albeit drummed up with unique accents reflecting the chef's distinctive style. The petite space is simple and lovely, with a modern-rustic décor and a genuinely cozy neighborhood vibe. A chef's counter in the back offers an up-close-and-personal kitchen experience.

Kick things off with the excellent Jonah crab salad, served with soft waffle-cut potato fritters and freshly made cocktail sauce. Then move on to the "pici with chew," thick strands of pici noodles cooked to a conservative al dente, and tossed with smoky bacon, chopped jalapeños, and breadcrumbs.

▨ 3209 W. Armitage Ave. (bet. Kedzie & Sawyer Aves.)
✆ (773) 252-0997 — **WEB:** www.giantrestaurant.com
▨ Dinner Tue – Sat   **PRICE:** $$

IXCATECO GRILL ⅋⅃

Mexican

✗ | ♿ BYO ⑤   **MAP:** B1

Servers stand erect as soldiers at Ixcateco Grill, their pressed white shirts tucked into immaculate black pants. It's a sight you wish you'd see more often—the unmistakable feeling that the staff cares deeply about your experience at this delicious Mexican hot spot. The colorful space, painted in bright shades of orange, green, and fuchsia, only adds to the bonhomie.

Chef Anselmo Ramírez, a veteran of Frontera Grill and Topolobampo, knows his way around Southern Mexican food. Try the irresistible picaditas, a pair of tender little masa canoes filled with savory chicken carnitas, pickled cactus, avocado cream, and queso fresco; or the wonderfully complex and authentic pollo en mole negro, sporting that perfect, complex blend of sweet and spicy mole.

▨ 3402 W. Montrose Ave. (bet. Bernard St. & Kimball Ave.)
🚇 Kedzie (Brown)
✆ (773) 539-5887 — **WEB:** www.ixcatecogrill.com
▨ Dinner Tue – Sun   **PRICE:** $$

JAM 😃
American

XX | & 🏠 🍴 📠

MAP: C3

Hiding in plain sight, Jam remains the sweetheart of brunch-o-philes who won't settle for some greasy spoon. White walls and stone tables punctuated by lime-green placemats give a gallery-like feel to the space; while a friendly welcome and open kitchen keep things homey.

Creative and refined versions of brunch favorites set this kitchen apart. For instance, French toast features brioche slices soaked in vanilla and malt-spiked custard, cooked sous vide, and then caramelized in a sizzling pan. Garnished with lime leaf-whipped cream and pineapple compote, this staple is sure to cure any hangover. Then braised beef and tomato crema are rolled into buckwheat crêpes and crowned by a sunny-side up egg for an elegant take on the breakfast burrito.

■ 3057 W. Logan Blvd. (at Albany Ave.)
🚇 Logan Square
📞 (773) 292-6011 — **WEB:** www.jamrestaurant.com
■ Lunch Thu – Tue

PRICE: 🍸

KAI ZAN 😃
Japanese

XX

MAP: C5

Despite doubling its space a few years ago, Kai Zan is still the kind of place that needs a reservation well in advance. Located on an otherwise solitary stretch of Humboldt Park, the space is particularly charming and makes you feel like you are stepping into a cozy neighborhood izakaya tucked away in a remote Japanese fishing hamlet. Savvy diners book a seat at the marble sushi counter to watch chefs and twin brothers Melvin and Carlo Vizconde perform their magic up close.

The brothers turn out sophisticated, creative dishes that are decked with myriad sauces, flavors and textures. Non-traditional sushi, nigiri, yakitori, as well as classic bar bites like takoyaki and karaage are all crafted with precise details and impeccable ingredients.

■ 2557 ½ W. Chicago Ave. (at Rockwell St.)
📞 (773) 278-5776 — **WEB:** www.eatatkaizan.com
■ Dinner Tue – Sat

PRICE: $$

LONGMAN & EAGLE 😊

Gastropub

🍴 | 🍸 🍺 ♿ 🏠 💺 📠

MAP: B3

Marked by a single ampersand over the door, Longman & Eagle is the ultimate merging of the Old World and New Order. It's where remnants of a glorious past live in harmony with chefs who prefer bandanas and beards to toques; and the cuisine remains as ambitious as ever despite the room's saloon-like feel.

Although lunch is rather limited, the kitchen remains particularly busy at all times and the cocktail program is nothing short of stellar. Creativity is at the center of each dish, including mortadella-stuffed agnolotti served with vibrant pea pureé and savory ham broth; or a block of deliciously flavored pork jowl coupled with Brussels sprouts, pommes pureé, and apple jus. Distinct desserts may reveal a tart key lime pie nicely balanced by sweet coconut cream.

◼ 2657 N. Kedzie Ave. (at Schubert Ave.)
◼ Logan Square
✆ (773) 276-7110 — **WEB:** www.longmanandeagle.com
◼ Lunch & dinner daily   **PRICE:** $$

L' PATRON 🍴

Mexican

🍴 | BYO 🍷 💵

MAP: B4

This local, no-frills and much-loved taqueria may have moved locations, but things remain largely the same. Signature lime-green and bright orange hues continue to decorate the interior space, which also features counter service, blaring bachata to keep you moving as you munch, and those wonderfully soft and flavorful homemade tortillas, tortas, tacos, and burritos.

Ultra-fresh dishes are assembled to order, like the taco al pastor, filled with sumptuous chunks of achiote-marinated pork and topped with chopped onion and cilantro. Then a version with carne asada may be offered, packed with grilled, well-seasoned beef; while crisp tortilla chips, still warm from the fryer, are addictive companions for scooping up chunky and garlicky guacamole.

◼ 3749 W. Fullerton Ave. (bet. Hamlin & Ridgeway Aves.)
✆ (773) 799-8066 — **WEB:** N/A
◼ Lunch & dinner Wed – Mon   **PRICE:** 🍴

LULA CAFE 😊

American

XX | ♿ 🛖 🍴 🖥   **MAP:** B3

This darling neighborhood staple is just as it's always been. No matter what's on the constantly evolving menu, the fresh, seasonal, and original fare keeps it slammed with Logan Square locals from morning to night.

Barbequed wedges of spaghetti squash topped with Asian pear, daikon, and sesame is impossible not to finish. Nicely grilled steaks are accompanied by a tangle of blistered long beans brushed in a house X.O. sauce with deliciously chewy bits of dried seafood for maximum umami flavor. Finish with a tall wedge of double-layered carrot cake complete with crème anglaise and a luxurious spoonful of strawberry preserves on the side. Come on Monday nights for their inspired Farm Dinners and get a taste of what is to come on the regular menu.

▨ 2537 N. Kedzie Ave. (off Logan Blvd.)
▨ Logan Square
✆ (773) 489-9554 — **WEB:** www.lulacafe.com
▨ Lunch & dinner Wed – Mon   PRICE: $$

MI TOCAYA 😊

Mexican

X | 🛖   **MAP:** C3

Boasting a lively, charming ambience; friendly, knowledgeable service; and a delicious menu courtesy of Chef/owner Diana Davila, Mi Tocaya is a welcome addition to the burgeoning Logan Square food scene. Bring friends, order a delicious seasonal cocktail, try something new from the menu, and you'll no doubt leave with a newfound love for Mexican cuisine.

The short but intriguing listing of "small cravings" (antojitos) is influenced by the less-explored Aztec cuisine of Mexico. Sample dishes like guisado de nopalitos, a fragrant, earthy stew with cactus, zucchini, and charred chilies, served with delicious knobs of salt-dusted fried cheese curds and warm corn tortillas. But don't overlook the warm tacos, sure to transport you to the streets of Mexico City.

▨ 2800 W. Logan Blvd. (at California Ave.)
▨ California (Blue)
✆ (872) 315-3947 — **WEB:** www.mitocaya.com
▨ Dinner Tue – Sun   PRICE: $$

NOON-O-KABAB ⅋⃝

Persian

XX | ♿

A bustling lunch crowd appreciates the welcoming hospitality at this family-run Persian favorite in the heart of the North Side. Intricate tilework and patterned wall hangings offset the closely spaced linen-topped tables and add touches of elegance to the homey space.

A basket of warm pita bread and a bowl of salty Bulgarian feta, parsley, and raw onions sate the appetites of those perusing the kababs on the menu. Succulent, hand-formed lamb koubideh and beef tenderloin skewers are juicy and charred with a hint of spice, and vegetarian offerings like tadiq with ghormeh sabzi play up the textural contrast of crispy pan-browned saffron rice against flavorful stewed spinach. Sample a glass of "awesome" house Earl Grey tea steeped with cardamom and ginger.

- 4661 N. Kedzie Ave. (at Leland Ave.)
- Kedzie (Brown)
- ℰ (773) 279-9309 — **WEB:** www.noonokabab.com
- Lunch & dinner daily

PRICE: 🫘

OSTERIA LANGHE ⅋⃝

Italian

XX | 🏨

MAP: C4

Osteria Langhe offers Logan Square a genuine taste of Italy—Piedmonte, to be exact. Partners Aldo Zaninotto and Chef Cameron Grant have created a sophisticated yet welcoming contemporary space, with warm, glowing bulbs that protrude from the walls, bare wood tables and metal chairs lining the floor. Additionally, a communal table at the restaurant's entrance, is visible through its garage-like glass façade.

The regionally focused food and wine list celebrates the Italian way of eating ("slow food") with legendary Piemontese pasta like the tajarin, a plate of deliciously eggy noodles twirled around savory ragù, diced carrots and bright green parsley. Dinner specials offer great value, most notably the Trifecta Tuesday $38 prix-fixe.

- 2824 W. Armitage Ave. (bet. California Ave. & Mozart St.)
- California (Blue)
- ℰ (773) 661-1582 — **WEB:** www.osterialanghe.com
- Dinner nightly

PRICE: $$

PARACHUTE ❀

Fusion

🍴 | ♿

MAP: B2

Husband-and-wife chef team Johnny Clark and Beverly Kim have put their little corner of Avondale on Chicago's culinary map with this hip and homey bistro. Young foodies fill the space every night, whether seated at tables lining the wooden banquette or perched along colorful stools dotting the double-sided counter that faces the open kitchen.

Though there's a distinctive Korean thread running through the menu, Parachute is a creative, open-ended endeavor at heart. Impeccably sourced ingredients from local purveyors lay the framework, but the team's brilliant application of cutting-edge techniques take the fare to inventive heights.

Baked potato bing bread, a signature flatbread carb-bomb, is stuffed with melted scallions and bacon bits, topped with sesame, and served with sour cream butter. The regularly re-written menu has also been known to feature tender braised pork shoulder with a fermented black bean- and dried shrimp-sauce, then paired with ripe figs and grilled pearl onion petals. Desserts make for a stellar finish. Order the patbingsu, which arrives in a pretty glass bowl layered with condensed milk ice cream, mochi rice cakes, concord grape shaved ice, Azuki beans, and toasted rice.

◾ 3500 N. Elston Ave. (at Troy St.)
☎ (773) 654-1460 — **WEB:** www.parachuterestaurant.com
◾ Dinner Tue – Sat   **PRICE:** $$

PARSON'S CHICKEN & FISH 🍽

American

 🍴 | 🍺 ♿ 🏕 📺 🛋   **MAP:** C4

For the young professionals and new families of gentrifying Logan Square, Parson's Chicken & Fish is a lively but low-key hangout that hits all the bases. It's equally appropriate for a midday snack with the kids or a late-night munchies run, and the stay-and-play vibe extends to on-site activities like a winter ice skating rink or summer ping pong tables.

As per the name, poultry and seafood offerings are house specialties, with signature golden-fried chicken (and equally popular Negroni slushies) on many tables. An aïoli-smeared brioche bun holds a piping-hot fillet of beer-battered fish topped with crisp slaw and house hot sauce. Dessert isn't made in house, but no matter; neighboring Bang Bang Pie Shop provides daily slices of sweetness.

- 2952 W. Armitage Ave. (at Humboldt Blvd.)
- California (Blue)
- (773) 384-3333 — **WEB:** www.parsonschickenandfish.com
- Lunch & dinner daily   **PRICE: $$**

QUIOTE 🙂

Mexican

XX | 🛋   **MAP:** C3

Logan Square may be buzzing with Mexican restaurants, but Quiote rises above them like a brightly hued piñata. Warm and inviting, with food that satisfies from sun up to sun down, this place embodies the very essence of a neighborhood spot.

While the menu's assortment of small and large plates is meant for sharing, the kitchen aims to please and will create a typical three-course meal upon request. Expect authentic Mexican fare with a creative twist, as evidenced by dishes such as the chorizo verde, a green-tinted pork sausage resting on smashed and griddled potatoes with sweet rings of onion and a golden raisin vinaigrette, or seasonally inspired plates like the flavorful crab tostada. As for what to drink? Three words: subterranean mezcal bar.

- 2456 N. California Ave. (at Altgeld St.)
- California (Blue)
- (312) 878-8571 — **WEB:** www.quiotechicago.com
- Lunch & dinner Wed – Mon   **PRICE: $$**

THE RADLER 🍴

German

🍴 | 🍺 ♿ 🚋 🍷   **MAP:** C4

With around 20 suds on tap and more than 95 bottles to sample, The Radler is everything you want in a beer hall. The restaurant may be young, but the space retains an old soul thanks to communal benches that harken back to the days of Bavarian biergartens. The enormous "Bohemian Export" beer mural that commands guests' attention is original to the building—a happy discovery during demolition. A stack of small plates on each table sends the message that everything on the menu is meant for sharing.

Food here may be crafted with drinking in mind, but that does not undermine its delicious creativity. Try the deep-golden pork loin schnitzel with bacon-braised lentils, dried Mission figs, and smoky cream sauce, balanced with a light green salad and charred lemon.

▦ 2375 N. Milwaukee Ave. (bet. California & Fullerton Aves.)
🚇 California (Blue)
☏ (773) 276-0270 — **WEB:** www.dasradler.com
▦ Lunch & dinner Tue – Sun   PRICE: $$

SHOKRAN MOROCCAN GRILL 🍴

Moroccan

🍴 | BYO 💵   **MAP:** A2

Embrace Moroccan hospitality to the fullest and bone up on your Arabic at Shokran, where the country's culinary culture is displayed in a romantic setting. Nooks and crannies throughout the dining rooms offer intimacy; take a seat among the cozy cushioned banquettes and prepare to say "shokran" (thank you) repeatedly as courses come your way.

Traditional dishes offer the most authentic experience, like sweet and savory bastilla, a flaky pastry starter that's large enough to serve two, stuffed with spiced chicken and dusted with cinnamon. Famously rustic, the lamb Marrakesh tagine features a meaty bone-in shank adorned with bitter slivers of preserved lemon and surrounded by sweet peas, whole black olives, and tender quartered artichoke hearts.

▦ 4027 W. Irving Park Rd. (bet. Keystone Ave. & Pulaski Rd.)
🚇 Irving Park (Blue)
☏ (773) 427-9130 — **WEB:** www.shokranchicago.com
▦ Dinner Wed – Mon   PRICE: 💰

SMOQUE BBQ 😋

Barbecue

X | ♿   **MAP:** A2

Smoque opens for lunch at 11:00 A.M., but a crowd of devotees can be found lining up for a barbecue fix long before then. Once inside, peruse the chalkboard menu, then order cafeteria-style before staking your claim among the communal seating while waiting (and salivating).

The half-and-half sandwich, piled with pulled pork and brisket, is the best of both worlds, with chunky shreds of tender pork and spice-rubbed slices of pink-rimmed beef spooned with vinegary barbecue sauce. The usual side dish suspects like zingy, crisp coleslaw and deeply smoky baked beans are anything but standard here, complementing the 'cue as they should. For a sweet finish, look no further than pecan bread pudding drizzled with salted caramel-Bourbon sauce.

▪ 3800 N. Pulaski Rd. (at Grace St.)
▪ Irving Park (Blue)
✆ (773) 545-7427 — **WEB:** www.smoquebbq.com
▪ Lunch & dinner Tue – Sun   **PRICE:** 🍜

SOL DE MEXICO 😋

Mexican

XX | ♿   **MAP:** A3

Far more authentic than the average chips-and-salsa joint, Sol de Mexico brightens the scene and palate with a lively atmosphere (cue the mariachi music!) and delectable house specialties. Walls painted in tropical pinks, blues, and oranges are a cheerful canvas for Dia de los Muertos artifacts. To sample the kitchen's skill, start with sopes surtidos "xilonen"—four molded masa cups with a variety of fillings like caramelized plantains doused in sour cream or tender black beans topped with crumbly house-made chorizo. Then, move on to the pollo en mole manchamanteles, which translates to "tablecloth stainer." Rich and slightly bitter with a comforting nuttiness, the aptly named mahogany sauce begs to be sopped up with freshly made tortillas.

▪ 3018 N. Cicero Ave. (bet. Wellington Ave. & Nelson St.)
✆ (773) 282-4119 — **WEB:** www.soldemexicochicago.com
▪ Lunch & dinner Wed – Mon   **PRICE:** $$

STAROPOLSKA ⫴○
Polish

✗ | ⬚

MAP: B3

Fans of traditional Polish cooking know to proceed to this Logan Square mainstay. If a stroll past nearby Kurowski's Sausage Shop doesn't put you in the mood for some meaty, belly-busting cuisine, then one step inside this Old World-style sanctum certainly will.

Polish pilsners and lagers are poured at the bar and pair perfectly with the stuffed and slow-cooked plates sent out by the kitchen. Pierogies are a staple, and are offered here with a variety of sweet and savory embellishments. Stuffed cabbage is available with a meatless mushroom filling, and house specialties include the placek po wegiersku: a light and tender griddled potato pancake folded over chunks of pork and bell pepper slices, braised in a tomato and sweet paprika sauce.

▦ 3030 N. Milwaukee Ave. (bet. Lawndale & Ridgeway Aves.)
✆ (773) 342-0779 — **WEB:** www.staropolskarestaurant.com
▦ Lunch & dinner daily

PRICE: ⌘

TABLE, DONKEY AND STICK ☻
Austrian

✗✗ | 🍺 & 🍴

MAP: C4

When American comfort food just won't suffice, look to Table, Donkey and Stick for a helping of cozy Alpine fare. The rustic inn-inspired setting reflects its reputation as a gathering place where friends meet at the inviting bar or settle in at communal tables for whimsical, creative compositions.

Though the food is European-influenced, ingredients from local farms make their way into many dishes. Caraway seeds spice up duck meatballs nestled among springy egg noodles with dehydrated sauerkraut and shaved salted egg yolk, and honeycomb tripe wins new fans when fried to a crisp and topped with house-made giardiniera. For a sweet take on the traditional baked good, try the pretzel-shaped puff pastry sprinkled with candied mustard seeds.

▦ 2728 W. Armitage Ave. (bet. California Ave. & North Point St.)
🚇 Western (Blue)
✆ (773) 486-8525 — **WEB:** www.tabledonkeystick.com
▦ Dinner nightly

PRICE: $$

LAKEVIEW & WRIGLEYVILLE

ROSCOE VILLAGE

Lakeview is the blanket term for the area north of Lincoln Park, including Roscoe Village and Wrigleyville (named after its iconic ball field). Keeping that in mind, enjoy a boisterous game with maximum conveniences at a Wrigley Field rooftop like **Murphy's Bleachers**, where hot dogs and hamburgers are washed down with pints of beer. When the beloved Cubs finish their season each October, don't despair, as these American summertime classics continue to shape the neighborhood's cuisine. Thanks to a large Eastern European population, a sumptuous supply of sausages and wursts can be found in a number of casual eateries or markets, including **Paulina**—a local institution where expected items like corned beef and lamb are offered beside more novel delights like ground venison and loin chops. This is also a hot spot among local Swedish families, who come for time-tested plates of pickled Christmas ham

or even cardamom-infused sausages. Other residents may opt to sojourn to **Ann Sather,** a sweet brunch spot branded for its baseball glove-sized cinnamon buns.

CLASSIC CHICAGO

Diners are all the craze in this area, starting with **Glenn's,** whose menu reads like a seafaring expedition with over 16 varieties of fish on offer. And between its kitchen's savory egg specialties, 30 types of cereal, and a blackboard menu that makes Egyptian tombs look brief, this is a veritable big city sort of spot and flaunts something for everyone. Similarly, the Windy City's passion for the humble hot dog is something to write home about, and Lakeview offers plenty of proof. Case in point—the dogs and burgers at **Murphy's Red Hots**, which may be simple in presentation, but are in fact amazing in taste. And keep in mind that this location has outdoor picnic tables and no inside seating.

BAKING IN BAVARIA

Even Chicagoans can't survive on hot dogs alone. Thankfully, Lakeview has an antidote for practically every craving imaginable. Should you have a hankering for Bavarian baked goods, for instance, **Dinkel's Bakery** is right around the corner. Originally opened by a master baker from Bavaria in 1922, this family-run business (in its current locale since 1932) is renowned for faithful renditions of strudels, butterkuchen, and stollen. Their big breakfast sandwich, the Dinkel's Burglaur, may be less traditional but is just as tasty—not unlike those decadent doughnuts. Items here can be purchased fresh, but are also available frozen for shipping to lucky out-of-town fans.

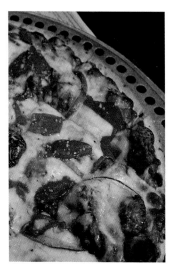

FASCINATING FOOD FINDS

For a different type of high, stop by south-of-the-border sensation, **5411 Empanadas**. This food truck-turned-storefront sells Argentinian empanadas with such inventive fillings as malbec beef or chorizo with *patatas bravas*. It also showcases impressive Latin sweets like *alfajores* to go with good, strong coffee. Connoisseurs of quality baked goods will want to pop into **Bittersweet Pastry Shop**, where luscious desserts have been crafted for almost two decades

now. It's a one-stop shop for everything from breads, pastries, and cupcakes, to exquisitely sculpted wedding confections. Those seeking a classic American experience should proceed to **The Roost Carolina Kitchen** for a 24-hour buttermilk-brined, hotter-than-hot take on the popular Southern fried hot chicken sandwich. Another laudation, even if it comes in buttery and sugary packages to these neighborhoods, is **City Caramels**, home to some lip-smacking treats. Settle in before making your way through Bucktown (by way of coffee-inspired caramels with chocolate-covered espresso beans); Lincoln Square (toasted hazelnuts anybody?), and Pilsen (Mexican drinking chocolate with ancho chili) along with their respective caramel and candy cuts. If savory bites are more your style, trek to **Pastoral**, commonly hailed as one of the country's top destinations for cheese. Their classic and farmstead varietals, fresh breads and olives, as well as intermittently scheduled tastings are a local treasure. An offbeat yet quirky vibe is part and parcel of Lakeview's fabric, and testament to this fact can be found at **The Flower Flat**, boasting a comforting breakfast or brunch repast in an actual flower shop. Meanwhile, **Uncommon Ground** is as much a restaurant serving three square meals a day as it is a coffee shop revered for its live music talent and performances. During the months between June and September, stop by at any time to admire their certified organic sidewalk garden before tasting its bounty on your plate, inside. And a few more blocks north, aspiring young chefs with big dreams proudly present a wholesome grab-n-go restaurant called **Real Kitchen**. Here on the menu, homestyle items like baked Amish chicken are paired with a unique and crusty pork belly sandwich to reflect each chef's take on a favored classic.

ROSCOE VILLAGE

Everyone loves a rollicking street fair, and this nabe's **Shock Top Oyster Fest** featuring an incredible music and beer selection, as well as worthy guests of honor (maybe a certain mollusk believed to have aphrodisiac qualities) doesn't disappoint. Nostalgic New Yorkers and transplants should take note: Roscoe Village is also home to **Apart Pizza**, Chicago's very own homage to the thin-crust pie. (Just remember, you're in deep-dish land, so you might want to refrain from admitting just how much you enjoyed it!) And finally, because no feast is complete without a bit of sweet, bide some time at **Scooter's Frozen Custard** whose creamy frozen delights are made fresh daily in a variety of flavors.

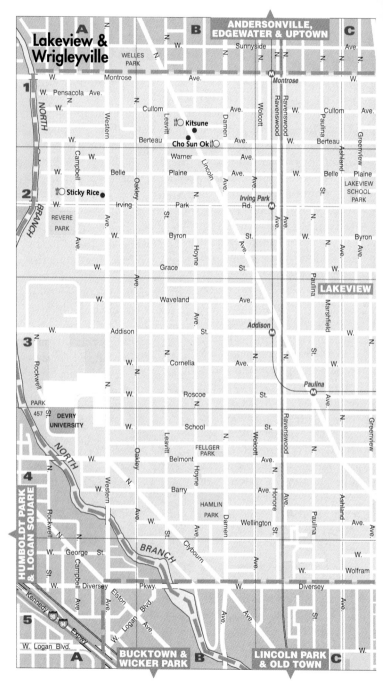

Lakeview & Wrigleyville

WELLES PARK

Sunnyside Ave.

W. Montrose Ave.   Montrose

W. Pensacola Ave.

Cullom Ave.   Cullom Ave.

Western   Leavitt   ‖○ **Kitsune**   Paulina   Greenview

W. Berteau Ave.   **Cho Sun Ok** ‖○   Berteau

W. Warner Ave.   Lincoln   Ashland

Campbell   Belle   Plaine Ave.   W. Belle   Plaine

Oakley   LAKEVIEW SCHOOL PARK

‖○ **Sticky Rice**   *Irving Park Rd.*   St.

W. Irving Park   **Irving Park**

REVERE PARK   St.   Ave.

W. Byron St.   W. Byron Ave.

Hoyne   Ave.   Ave.

Grace St.   W.

Ave.   Paulina   **LAKEVIEW**

W. Waveland Ave.   Marshfield

Ave.   W.

Addison St.   *Addison*

W. Cornelia Ave.   St.

Rockwell   W. Roscoe St.   *Paulina*   Ave.

PARK   457   St.

DEVRY UNIVERSITY   W. School St.   Ravenswood   Greenview

Leavitt   FELLGER PARK   Wolcott

Oakley   Belmont Ave.

NORTH   Hoyne   Honore   Paulina   Ashland

W. Barry Ave.

Western   HAMLIN PARK   Damen   Wellington   Ave.

BRANCH   Clybourn   Wolfram

Rockwell   Campbell   W. George St.   W. Diversey

W. Diversey Pkwy.   Elston   Logan   Ave.   Ave.   St.

Kennedy   90   94   Expwy.

W. Logan Blvd.   W.

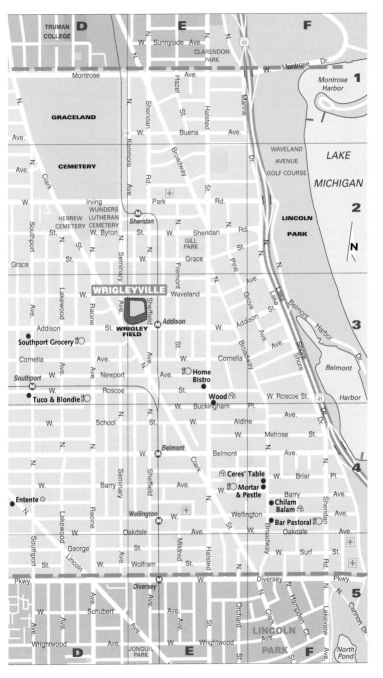

TRUMAN
COLLEGE

D

E

F

W. Sunnyside Ave.

CLARENDON
PARK

41

W. Montrose   Dr.

Montrose   Ave.

Montrose
Harbor

1

GRACELAND

W. Buena   Ave.

WAVELAND

CEMETERY

AVENUE

LAKE

GOLF COURSE

MICHIGAN

Ave.

Irving   Park   Rd.

WUNDERS

LINCOLN

HEBREW   LUTHERAN

N

CEMETERY   CEMETERY

PARK

W. Byron   St.

Sheridan

2

W. Sheridan   Rd.

GILL
PARK

Grace   St.

Grace

W. Waveland

WRIGLEYVILLE

Addison   W. Addison   Ave.

● Southport Grocery ‖○

**WRIGLEY
FIELD**

Cornelia

Cornelia   Ave.

Southport   W. Newport   Ave.   ‖○ **Home
Bistro**

● **Tuco & Blondie** ‖○   W. Roscoe   St.   **Wood** ⊕   W. Roscoe St.   41

Harbor

W. Buckingham   Pl.

W. School   St.   W. Aldine   Ave.

W. Melrose   St.

● **Entente** ✿   W. Belmont   Belmont   Ave.

⊕ **Ceres' Table**   W. Briar   Pl.

W ‖○ **Mortar
& Pestle**   Barry   Ave.

Wellington   W.   ● **Chilam
Balam** ⊕

● **Bar Pastoral** ‖○

W. Oakdale   Ave.   Wellington   Oakdale   Ave.

George   St.

Lincoln   W. Wolfram   St.

Pkwy.   *Diversey*   W.   Diversey   Pkwy.

5

W. Schubert   Ave.   **LINCOLN**

PARK

W. Wrightwood   Ave.   JONQUIL   W. Wrightwood   Ave.

D   PARK   **E**   **F**   *North
Pond*

BAR PASTORAL 🍴

International

🍱 | ⛱ ⚞   **MAP:** F4

With a cheese selection that spans the globe and charcuterie flaunting the best in the Midwest, this is a prized haunt among urbanites craving some wine with their savory eats. Subtly styled like a cave for aging, its barrel-vaulted ceilings and exposed brick walls evoke intimacy. A half-moon bar, marble-topped cheese counter, and wood tables let guests gather and sample.

As expected, many dishes feature cheese, though larger and shareable plates "from the kitchen" range from simple (roasted garlic plate) to complex (rack of lamb). Thick slices of bacon-wrapped country pâté are studded with pistachios. And, a concise wine list offers unique options for coupling with cheese, of course—the raw cow's milk Kentucky Rose with onion chutney is thoroughly delicious.

🔲 2947 N. Broadway (bet. Oakdale & Wellington Aves.)
🚇 Wellington
📞 (773) 472-4781 — **WEB:** www.pastoralartisan.com
🔲 Lunch Sat – Sun Dinner nightly   **PRICE:** $$

CERES' TABLE 😊

Italian

✗✗ | ♿ ⛱ ⚞   **MAP:** F4

Ceres' Table continues its reign as a stylish setting for enjoying the kitchen team's rustic Italian cooking. Whether waking up with brunch, snacking at aperitivo hour, or filling up with the $22 trio (pizza, beer, and dessert), there's an excuse to stop in for any occasion or budget.

Seasonal Italian-inspired cuisine offering elegantly rustic dishes made with solid skill is represented throughout the menu. Here, find a wood-burning oven turning out a range of first-rate pizzas as well as mains like a perfectly grilled whole branzino set on a plate and topped with a heaping pile of lightly dressed salad greens and shaved radish. For sweet simplicity, try the Tuscan torta della nonna with buttery baby pine nuts coating a wedge of vanilla-tinged custard pie.

🔲 3124 N. Broadway (bet. Barry Ave. & Briar Pl.)
🚇 Belmont (Brown/Red)
📞 (773) 922-4020 — **WEB:** www.cerestable.com
🔲 Lunch Sun Dinner Tue – Sun   **PRICE:** $$

CHILAM BALAM 😎

Mexican

✗ | [BYO] [S]

Chilam Balam's cozy subterranean space feels like an undiscovered hideaway, but the secret of this lively Mexican hot spot is out. Though waits can be long, the accommodating staff goes the extra mile to mix up margaritas with BYO tequila or walk guests through the rotating roster of shared plates.

Familiar favorites and seasonal specials make for a festive mix of adventurous, yet universally pleasing dishes. Flat corn tortillas form a sandwich-style enchilada, stuffed with fork-tender beef brisket and topped with crunchy strands of sweet potato slaw. Salty chorizo and green papaya tlacoyos show that opposites attract, and peanut butter empanadas—primed for dipping in Oaxacan chocolate sauce and dulce de leche—take a childhood favorite to new heights.

▪ 3023 N. Broadway (bet. Barry & Wellington Aves.)
▪ Wellington
✆ (773) 296-6901 — **WEB:** www.chilambalamchicago.com
▪ Dinner Tue – Sat   **PRICE:** $$

CHO SUN OK 🍴

Korean

✗ | [BYO]

As tempted as you might be to judge this book by its brisk, unsmiling cover, don't. Instead, enter the cozy, wood-paneled den and raise that first delicious forkful to your mouth.

Take a cue from the regulars and start with galbi, a crave-worthy signature that glistens from a sweet and garlicky soy marinade and warrants good old-fashioned finger-licking. Haemul pajeon stuffed with squid and scallions is a crisp, golden-fried delight; and kimchi jjigae is a rich, bubbling, and nourishing broth packed with soft tofu and tender pork. Summer calls for a taste of the bibim naengmyeon—a chilled broth floating with buckwheat noodles, fresh veggies, Asian pear, and crimson-red gochujang all tossed together for a delicious reprieve from the city's sweltering heat.

▪ 4200 N. Lincoln Ave. (at Berteau Ave.)
▪ Irving Park (Brown)
✆ (773) 549-5555 — **WEB:** www.chosunokrestaurant.com
▪ Lunch & dinner daily   **PRICE:** ⌾

ENTENTE ✿

Contemporary

XX | &

With its striking glass façade and moody interior, this lovely sanctum makes quite an impression along North Lincoln Avenue. Entente's talented team is to thank for its creative American culinary vision, and the contemporary menu—designed for sharing and well worth exploring with friends—is unabashedly authentic and interesting.

The space is composed of two dining rooms: one up front with dark floors and ceilings, and another in the back with a full view of the bustling kitchen. A bar area featuring a high wall adorned with backlit wood boxes (which shelve the spirits) offers yet another spot to sample the delicious food.

Each dish delivers a remarkable mouthful, and most of the kitchen's creations are rich as well as unexpected (imagine green garbanzo hummus, paired with savory falafel, grilled apricots and pillowy flatbread tucked with apricot and nuts). Perfectly cooked pork loin arrives tender as butter, plated with cornbread purée, fragrant sweet tea jam, cornbread studded with huitlacoche, ribbons of braised collard greens, and crispy pork belly. Seafood lovers will leave smitten by the green curry—dotted with poached lobster and served with pickled cucumbers and coconut flakes.

▨ 3056 N. Lincoln Ave. (bet. Barry & Wellington Aves.)
☏ (872) 206-8553 — **WEB:** www.ententechicago.com
▨ Dinner Tue – Sat   PRICE: $$$

HOME BISTRO 🍴

American

✗✗ | 🛋 BYO

Home dishes up loads of charm with a healthy dash of humor in the heart of Boystown. Flickering tea lights on the closely packed bistro-style tables faintly illuminate cozy orange walls painted with food-related quotes. Chef Victor Morenz's eclectic menu picks up influences from around the globe, but each dish is consistently gratifying.

Southern meets south of the border in crisp fried oyster tacos with pickled pepper remoulade. Candied kumquats and olive tapenade contrast pleasantly with buttery seared duck breast, and a dense cube of warm, fudgy chocolate cake placed over a swipe of coconut peanut butter is a decadent finale. Plan for an early evening if you're looking forward to a quiet meal; at peak hours, those orange walls really reverberate.

■ 3404 N. Halsted St. (at Roscoe St.)
🚇 Belmont (Brown/Red)
✆ (773) 661-0299 — **WEB:** www.homebistrochicago.com
■ Lunch Sun Dinner Tue – Sun   **PRICE: $$**

KITSUNE 🍴

Fusion

✗ | 🛋

Kitsune is what happens when a Michelin-starred chef opens up shop in a remote corner of Lakeview. Chef Iliana Regan works serious magic in this kitchen, tossing in sprinkles of Midwestern ingredients as well as a liberal dose of wonderful wackiness with Japanese-inspired izakaya cooking. Familiar and surprising at once, the resulting dishes are immensely popular with the area's young foodie crowd.

Sink your teeth into thick slices of wild rice and koji porridge bread spread with house-cultured butter. Then dig into their heartwarming chawanmushi, a steamed egg custard topped with sweet Jonah crab; or slurp up the shoyu ramen, a delicious tangle of stinging nettle noodles, yuzu-marinated sea beans, and grilled negi in a vegan dashi broth.

■ 4229 N. Lincoln Ave. (at Hutchinson St.)
✆ N/A — **WEB:** www.kitsunerestaurant.com
■ Lunch Sat – Sun Dinner Tue – Sun   **PRICE: $$**

MORTAR & PESTLE 🍴

International

🍴 | 🖥 🔥 BYO   **MAP:** F4

This charming neighborhood brunch spot arrives courtesy of Chefs Stephen Ross and Stephen Paul, who worked together at Table 52. The farmhouse-designed space is rustic, welcoming, and full of personal touches, like reclaimed wood tables and vintage stained glass windows. And the service is genuinely friendly—coffee is poured the minute you sit down, and the chefs often appear to greet guests in person.

The kitchen's slogan is "globally inspired cuisine, rooted in tradition" and their globe-trotting ingredients—merguez sausage, cheese curds, romesco sauce—wind their way into a delicious array of brunchy items. Standards like eggs Benedict and French toast get sweet elevation from unexpected, upscale elements like King crab or even foie gras torchon.

🔲 3108 N. Broadway (at Barry Ave.)
🏠 Wellington
📞 (773) 857-2087 — **WEB:** www.mortarandpestlechicago.com
🔲 Lunch Wed – Mon   **PRICE:** 💰

SOUTHPORT GROCERY 🍴

American

🍴 | 🖥 🔥   **MAP:** D3

Equal parts specialty grocery and upscale diner, this Southport Corridor hot spot draws quite a crowd. Local products and in-house goodies are stocked in the front of the narrow space, while the rear offers comfortable banquettes for a casual sit-down meal.

Breakfast is served as long as the sun shines, with options like a freshly baked and buttered English muffin stuffed with ginger-sage sausage, a vibrant orange sunny side-up egg, and sweet pepper jelly. A side of red bliss potatoes sweetens the deal, but if you're really looking for something sugary, the grilled coffee cake is a double-layered cinnamon and cream cheese delight. Craving more of your meal? You're in luck: certain menu items, denoted with an asterisk, are available for purchase up front.

🔲 3552 N. Southport Ave. (bet. Addison St. & Cornelia Ave.)
🏠 Southport
📞 (773) 665-0100 — **WEB:** www.southportgrocery.com
🔲 Lunch daily   **PRICE:** 💰

STICKY RICE 🍴

Thai

✂ | BYO

There's no dearth of Thai joints in this neighborhood, but Sticky Rice stands out—not only for its focus on Northern Thai specialties, but also for the quality and abundance of dishes made to order. Sunny and citrus-hued, it's the kind of place where those who dare to step outside their satay-and-pad Thai comfort zone will be greatly rewarded.

Luckily, the extensive menu makes it easy to do just that. Tender egg noodles absorb the fragrant coconut curry in a bowl of kow soy that's redolent of citrusy coriander and served with pickled greens and cilantro. Duck larb is zippy and full of spice, with an unforgettable tart-and-sweet dressing. Hint: use the spot's namesake sticky rice to temper the heat while soaking up every last drop.

- 4018 N. Western Ave. (at Cuyler Ave.)
- Irving Park (Blue)
- (773) 588-0133 — **WEB:** www.stickyricethai.com
- Lunch & dinner daily

PRICE: 🍜

TUCO & BLONDIE 🍴

Mexican

✂✂ | 🍸 ♿ 🏠 🛷

MAP: D3

Solid Tex-Mex fare, killer margaritas, and a soft-serve ice cream machine in the window—what's not to love about this cheerful restaurant, with its brick walls, dramatic murals, and inviting outdoor courtyard complete with a huge, toasty fireplace?

Grab a seat—outside if you can swing it—and dig into a crowd-pleasing starter like the chili con queso "Bob Armstrong," basically a chili-laced cheese sauce bumped up with ground beef, guacamole and sour cream. Then move on to a mouthwatering taco trio, starring chili-braised short rib, grilled mahi mahi or chicken tinga; or the perfectly prepared steak fajitas, joined by sautéed peppers and charred jalapeño. Paired with fresh flour tortillas, cilantro rice, and homemade refried beans, this is Tex-Mex nirvana.

- 3358 N. Southport Ave. (at Roscoe St.)
- Southport
- (773) 327-8226 — **WEB:** www.tucoandblondie.com
- Lunch & dinner daily

PRICE: $$

WOOD 😊

Contemporary

XX | 🍹 ♿ 🛋 �

MAP: E3

You might think everyone comes to Wood for the great music and cheeky cocktail list (Strictly Platonic, anyone?), or even the audaciously dubbed "Morning Wood" brunch on weekends. But really, it's Chef Ashlee Aubin's menu that keeps this sleek dining space packed every night. Generous portions and that irresistibly lively atmosphere (a little bit sophisticated, a little bit disco) only seal the deal.

Aubin has crafted a rotating, seasonal menu that's concise but packs a hefty punch. Imagine wood-oven flatbreads, topped with fennel sausage and wilted greens, melt-in-your-mouth steak tartare, or tangles of spaghetti con vongole. Dinner on the other hand might involve a juicy bone-in pork chop, hearty cheeseburger, tender roasted chicken, or seared scallops.

◼ 3335 N. Halsted St. (at Buckingham Pl.)

🚇 Belmont (Brown/Red)

📞 (773) 935-9663 — **WEB:** www.woodchicago.com

◼ Lunch Sat – Sun   Dinner nightly

PRICE: $$

Look for our symbol 🍺
spotlighting restaurants
with a notable beer list.

LINCOLN PARK & OLD TOWN

The congregation of history, commerce, and nature is what makes Lincoln Park and Old Town one of Chicago's most iconic districts. Scenically situated on Lake Michigan's shore, the eponymous park offers winter-weary locals an excuse to get out. And if that isn't enticing enough, the park also keeps its patrons happy with a spectacular array of cafés, restaurants ranging from quick bites to the city's most exclusive reservations, and takeout spots offering picnic-perfect products. Populated by college grads, young families, and wealthy upstarts, as well as home to more than a handful of historic districts, museums, shopping, music venues, and the famous (not to mention, free) zoo, Lincoln Park flourishes as a much sought-after destination year-round.

DELICIOUS DINING

Wallet-happy locals and well-heeled gourmands make reservations to come here and dine at some of the most exclusive restaurants in town. But beyond just glorious white-glove dining destinations, there's more

delicious eating to be done in this area. During the weekend, these streets are jumping thanks to a combination of plays, musicals, bars, and scores of high-rises housing affluent and brash yuppies. On Wednesdays and Saturdays during the **Green City Market**, the south end of the park is transformed into hipster chef-cum-foodie central. With the aim to increase availability of top produce and to improve the link between farmers and local producers with restaurants and food organizations, this market works to educate the Windy City's masses about high-quality food sourcing. (In winter it is held across the street inside the Peggy Notebaert Nature Museum).

Lincoln Park's outpost of **Floriole Café & Bakery** brought about much jubilation, and along with it, a regular fan following. In fact, the aromas wafting from freshly baked breads, pastries, and cookies never fail to tempt onlookers. For the recreational chef, **Read it & Eat** is a kitchen workshop that doubles as a fully stocked bookstore housing a fantastic selection of cookbooks. Check out their calendar of food-centric events— from informative hands-on classes to drool-worthy book launches. Like many foods (Juicy Fruit, Cracker Jack, and Shredded Wheat, for example), it is said that the Chicago-style dog may have originated at the Chicago World's Fair and Columbian Exhibition in 1893. Others credit the Great Depression for its birth. Regardless of its origin, the prolific Chicago-style dog can be found at dog stalls all over the city. One such stand is **Chicago's Dog House**, offering nearby DePaul students, as well as the neighborhood, a range of classic and specialty creations. Similarly, **The Wieners Circle** is as known and loved for its delicious dogs and fries, late hours (as late as 5:00 A.M.), and intentionally rude service. Red meat fiends may

choose to carry on the party at **Butcher & the Burger** as they do their part to stay at the helm of the burger game, or linger at **Gepperth's Meat Market**, which was established in 1906 when the neighborhood was comprised of mostly Hungarian and German settlers. Old-world butchery is the dictum here with knowledge that has been passed down for generations. If prime cuts and all the trimmings come to mind, you know you've arrived at the right place. Meanwhile the ocean's bounty can be relished in all its glory at **Half Shell**. Here, the cash-only policy has done nothing to deter crowds from consuming platters of crab legs and briny oysters. Wash down these salty treats with a cool sip from a choice selection at **Goose Island Brewery**—makers of the city's favorite local beers. Keep up this alcohol-fueled fun at **Barrelhouse Flat**, which is always hip and happening thanks to a litany of hand-crafted punches. Then wind up in time (for happy hour perhaps?) at **The Drinkingbird**. From a sweet and stirring sake punch to spicy, homemade sausages, their carte du jour is nothing less than satisfying.

Lincoln Park is also one of the most dog-friendly areas around, but then what else would you expect from a neighborhood named after a huge expanse of grass? Big bellies and bold palates with Fido in tow are forever filling up on artisanal goods at **Blue Door Farm Stand**. This particularly edgy grocery-cum-café also doubles as a watering hole and breakfast hot spot for lunching ladies who can be found picking at kale salads or indulging in grilled cheese sammies. If that doesn't bring a smile, the deep-fried oreos at **Racine Plumbing** or decadent popcorn from **Berco's** boutique will certainly do the trick. To keep that sugar rush going, **Cocoa + Co.** is a chocoholic's dream. This candy shop and café stocks a heavenly collection of chocolate eats and pastries from around the world, as well as comforting cups of hot cocoa and coffee. Feeling those sugar blues? Burn off the calories with a good

laugh at The Second City, the country's foremost comedy club.

The Old Town quarter has a few quaint cobblestoned streets that are home to the Second City comedy scene (now with a Zanies, too, for even more laughs). Also nestled here is June's annual must-see (and must-shop) Old Town Art Fair; the Wells Street Art Fair; as well as places to rest with beers and a groovy jukebox—including the **Old Town Ale House**. However, Wells Street is the neighborhood's main drag, and is really where browsing should begin. Any epicurean shopping trip should also include **The Spice House** for its exotic spice blends, many named after local landmarks; or **Old Town Oil** for hostess gifts like infused oils and aged vinegars. Prefer a sweeter vice? **The Fudge Pot** tempts with windows of toffee, fudge, and other chocolate-y decadence. Lastly, you may not be a smoker, but the Up Down Cigar is worth a peek for its real cigar store Indian carving.

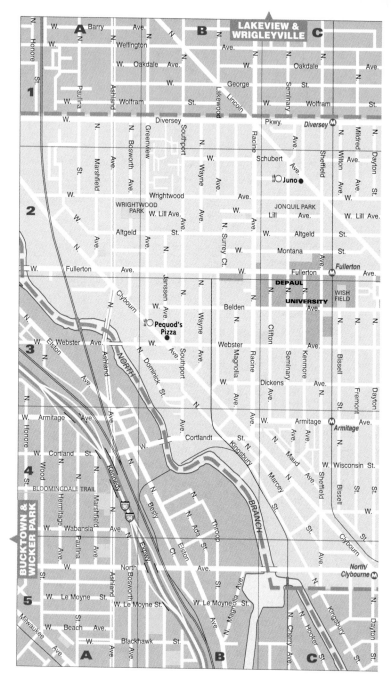

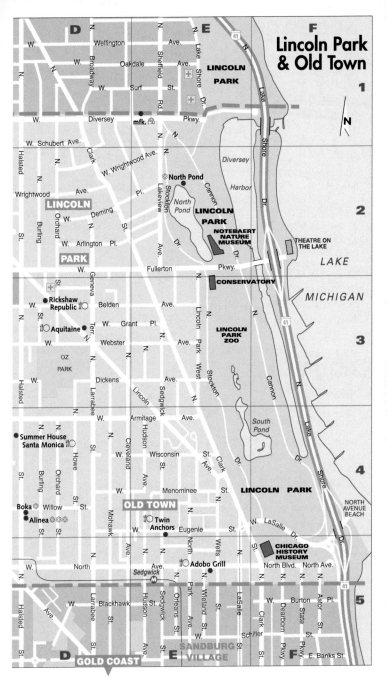

Lincoln Park & Old Town

D   **E**   **F**

N

Wellington   Ave.
N.
Broadway   Oakdale   Ave.
W.   Surf   St.
Sheffield   **LINCOLN**
Lake   **PARK**
Shore
W.   Diversey   **mfk.**   Rd.   Pkwy.   **1**

W. Schubert Ave.
Clark
W. Wrightwood Ave.   N.   *Diversey*
Halsted   Wrightwood   Ave.   Pl.   ● North Pond   *Harbor*
Stockton
Lakeview
N.
Orchard   Deming   North   **LINCOLN**
Burling   W.   Pond   **PARK**
LINCOLN   Geneva   W. Arlington Pl.   Dr.   **NOTEBAERT**
St.   **NATURE**
PARK   W.   Fullerton   **MUSEUM**   **2**
THEATRE ON
THE LAKE

● **Rickshaw**
Republic   Belden   Ave.   **CONSERVATORY**
W.   **LAKE**
● **Aquitaine**   Terr.   W. Grant Pl.
Webster   Lincoln   **MICHIGAN**
OZ   Larrabee   Park   **LINCOLN**   Cannon
PARK   Dickens   Ave.   **PARK**   **3**
Halsted   Lincoln   Sedgwick   West   **ZOO**
Stockton

Armitage   Ave.
● **Summer House**   Hudson   *South*
Santa Monica   Cleveland   Wisconsin   St.   *Pond*   **4**
Howe   Burling   Orchard   Ave.   Clark
St.   W.   Menominee   St.   **LINCOLN PARK**
● **Boka**   Willow   St.   **OLD TOWN**   **NORTH**
● **Alinea**   St.   Mohawk   ● **Twin**   **AVENUE**
Anchors   Eugenie   St.   **BEACH**
W.   North   ● **Adobo Grill**   Wells   **CHICAGO**
Ave.   *Sedgwick*   St.   North Blvd.   **HISTORY**
Halsted   Larrabee   Hudson   Sedgwick   Orleans   Park   Wieland   LaSalle   **MUSEUM**
W.   Blackhawk   St.   St.   Ave.   St.   W.   Burton   Astor   Pl.   **5**
Clark   Dearborn   State   Pkwy.
Schiller   St.
SANDBURG   St.
GOLD COAST   **VILLAGE**   E. Banks St.
D   **E**   **F**

ADOBO GRILL ¶⚪

Mexican

XX | 🍸 ⚐ 🏠 🗻

A fire may have caused their move within Old Town, but their margaritas are still shaken tableside and better than ever. The space is tastefully decorated with dark wood, rich red walls hung with Mexican paintings, and a welcoming back patio. Many remember Adobo for its tasty drinks, but the cooking is just as adept.

Guacamole is mashed to-order before your eyes, with just the right amount of jalapeños to suit your preference. Other dishes show a bit of fusion, like the ceviche de atun made with sashimi-grade tuna tossed with cucumbers, serrano chilies, and creamy avocado in ginger-soy sauce. Tacos al pastor offer tender chunks of roasted pork and caramelized pineapple topping fresh corn tortillas. Desserts are pleasantly traditional.

　 215 W. North Ave. (bet. Wells & Wieland Sts.)
　 Sedgwick
　 (312) 266-7999 — **WEB:** www.adobogrill.com
　 Lunch Sun Dinner nightly   PRICE: $$

AQUITAINE ¶⚪

American

XX | ⚐

When Lincoln Park locals want French-inspired cuisine, they head to Aquitaine for a taste of Chef/owner Holly Willoughby's refined cooking. Dim lighting and subtle brocade details on the walls keep the long, narrow dining room casually romantic, with enough simple sophistication to swing a Saturday night date or weekday post-work dinner. A well-priced wine list only adds to the elegant appeal.

Large chunks of succulent lobster are a luxe touch in a ramekin of potato gnocchi bathed in a rich pea-studded sauce. Eggplant, olive, and tomato relish gives double-cut lamb chops a Provençal spin, heightened by a drizzle of basil pesto. Textbook-perfect crème brûlée needs only a tap of the spoon to send its delicate sugar crust splintering into the silken custard.

　 2221 N. Lincoln Ave. (bet. Belden & Webster Aves.)
　 Fullerton
　 (773) 698-8456 — **WEB:** www.aquitainerestaurant.com
　 Dinner nightly   PRICE: $$

ALINEA ✿✿✿

Contemporary

XxxX | 🕸 ♿ ⬜ 🤚

Billed as a reinvention but what in reality was more a renovation, Alinea 2.0 is no longer a freewheeling circus of culinary showmanship. The entire space is now more subdued, with fewer stunts and minimal pomp. It offers maturity, substance, soul, and a level of infectious confidence unknown in its previous incarnation. This restaurant is more about you (the guest) than them (Chef Grant Achatz and his deeply talented team). Service, too, has never been more attentive and engaged, thanks to a staff who brings both humor and personality to the meal.

The menu style has been completely revamped, so even the most frequent visitor will have some surprises in store. There are three seating options, each with its own menu. The Salon is the most modest with eleven courses, while the Gallery offers a few more dishes with copious bells and whistles. The third and most opulent is the Kitchen Table, where outright bacchanalia ensues for a price tag that will probably leave Nick Kokonas the only one smiling. (Actual prices vary according to the date and time of your pre-paid reservation.)

Highlights are always whimsical, sometimes experimental, and may include scented vapors, smoke, and balloons.

◼ 1723 N. Halsted St. (bet. North Ave. & Willow St.)
🚇 North/Clybourn
✆ (312) 867-0110 — **WEB:** www.alinearestaurant.com
◼ Dinner Wed – Sun   **PRICE: $$$$**

BOKA ✿
Contemporary

XxX | 🍸 ♿ 🏠 🖨 🧼

This is the kind of place where one can sink in and never leave. The three dining rooms each exude elegance with a bit of romance and quirk, thanks to walls covered in ornate escutcheons and whimsical paintings. Against these dark pebbled backgrounds, find oversized booths, banquettes, and mirrored light bulbs casting funky shadows. The semi-outdoor solarium also has a living wall of moss and ferns. Servers are friendly, genuine and without a hint of pretense.

Chef Lee Wolen's modern menu is widely appealing with a Mediterranean edge. Meals are designed for guests to choose one hot and one cold appetizer, like yellowtail slices over fennel, dotted with the flavored oils and emulsions of horseradish, pistachio, and Concord grape. This might be followed by campanelle strewn with chanterelles, deboned frog legs, porcini mushroom powder, and pecorino. Main courses have included a graceful preparation of olive oil-poached walleye with white matsutake mushroom sabayon and roasted sunchokes.

In the same vein, dessert is an exceptionally pleasant experience. Fromage blanc beignets, for instance, are rolled in sugar, wattleseed, and set over diced pear, pear sorbet and flower petals.

▨ 1729 N. Halsted St. (bet. North Ave. & Willow St.)

🚇 North/Clybourn

✆ (312) 337-6070 — **WEB:** www.bokachicago.com

▨ Dinner nightly

PRICE: $$$

JUNO ᵗᵗ◯

Japanese

XX | ◌˗   **MAP:** C2

Raw fish with a side of creativity differentiates Juno from the rest of this city's sushi brethren. Inside, a rather plain and dimly lit bar up front gives way to the more contemporary, bright and airy dining room, which is a huge hit among locals looking to get all dressed-up for a night out. The menu offers cool bites like the Juno queen, a special nigiri of salmon topped with scallop and potato crunch; and hot treats like honey-glazed quail.

Chef B.K. Park's omakase must be ordered 24 hours in advance. Try cleverly spun morsels like gently torched prawn with pineapple salsa, pickled garlic oil-drizzled New Zealand King salmon, soy-marinated sea eel dabbed with ground sesame seeds, and spicy octopus temaki—it's a feast well worth the extra effort.

▦ 2638 N. Lincoln Ave. (bet. Seminary & Sheffield Aves.)
▦ Diversey
✆ (773) 935-2000 — **WEB:** www.junosushichicago.com
▦ Dinner Tue – Sun   **PRICE:** $$$

MFK. ☻

Spanish

X   **MAP:** E1

"First we eat, then we do everything else," said M.F.K. Fisher, the food writer who serves as both the inspiration and namesake for this young neighborhood darling. Thanks to large windows, whitewashed brick walls, and gleaming silver-and-white tilework, the subterranean space manages to evoke a breezy seaside oasis. And with a seafood-centric menu featuring modern interpretations of Iberian-inspired plates, the food follows suit.

The ocean's bounty is showcased in simple but flavorful dishes like crispy fried prawn heads served with a nutty salbitxada sauce for dipping; and bowls of cataplana stew with fresh clams, crunchy shrimp, and grilled cobia collar. A crumbly slice of Basque cake and an expertly pulled cortado end the meal on a high note.

▦ 432 W. Diversey Pkwy. (bet. Pine Grove Ave. & Sheridan Rd.)
▦ Diversey
✆ (773) 857-2540 — **WEB:** www.mfkrestaurant.com
▦ Lunch Wed – Sun   Dinner nightly   **PRICE:** $$

NORTH POND ✿

Contemporary

XX | 🦋 🖼 🛋 🖫

This charming Arts and Crafts building may have started as a warming shelter for park ice skaters back in 1912, but today it is a celebratory and cozy setting that makes you want to light a fire and pop open some champagne. Exposed brick, that roaring fireplace, and large windows overlooking the park and lake make the rooms feel warm and pleasant.

A commitment to agriculture is clear in everything: seed packets arrive with the check and each bottle of wine has a one-dollar surcharge that is donated to charities like the Lincoln Park Conservancy or Chicago Rarities Orchard Project.

Chef Bruce Sherman has a particular style that almost seems to fly in the face of those minimalist competitors who use menus to list single ingredients. Here, dishes are described comprehensively as a flurry of ingredients that may not seem to fit together, but they always do with great success. Try neatly trimmed Arctic char that is slow-roasted for silken texture, then served with embellishments like house-made sauerkraut, mustard seeds, candied walnuts, and Dauphine potatoes. A duo of strip steak and spoon-tender Porter-braised short rib arrives with pan-crisped black pepper spaetzle, Brussels sprouts, and beet-apple purée.

🔲 2610 N. Cannon Dr.
✆ (773) 477-5845 — **WEB:** www.northpondrestaurant.com
🔲 Lunch Sun   Dinner Wed – Sun   **PRICE: $$$**

PEQUOD'S PIZZA ⍨○

Pizza

✗ | ⚹   **MAP:** B3

Ditch your diet, grab your fellow Blackhawks fans, and head to this Lincoln Park stalwart for some of the best pies in town. Christened for Captain Ahab's sailing ship, Pequod's menu promises smooth sailing for sports bar noshers, featuring a lineup of shareable bar snacks such as wings and mozzarella sticks, hearty sandwiches like tender Italian beef, and both thin-crust and deep-dish pan pizzas.

Grab that cutlery before digging into the buttery crust of each deep-dish pie, ringed with blackened cheese at the edges. Toppings like pepperoni, fresh garlic, and crunchy sautéed onions are generously layered between tart tomato sauce and handfuls of cheese for an oozy jumble in every bite. A towering wedge of fudge cake awaits those with room for dessert.

▮ 2207 N. Clybourn Ave. (at Webster Ave.)
▮ Armitage
✆ (773) 327-1512 — **WEB:** www.pequodspizza.com
▮ Lunch & dinner daily   **PRICE:** ⊚⊚

RICKSHAW REPUBLIC ⍨○

Indonesian

✗ | ⚹ **BYO**   **MAP:** D3

The captivating flavors of Southeast Asian street food are matched by the creative design at this friendly, family-run Lincoln Avenue space. Color and pattern collide as parasols, puppets, and bird cages vie for attention with abstract Indonesian wood carvings. Once the food arrives, though, the spotlight shifts to the aromatic plates.

Start with crisp martabak crêpes that hold a savory combination of beef, onions, and egg. Then move on to lemongrass-braised chicken thighs in a turmeric-tinged coconut curry with sweet and spicy tamarind sambal and pickled cabbage. Surprise your palate with es cendol, a mix of coconut milk and green pandan jelly in palm sugar syrup. Finally, take one of Mama Setiawan's homemade sambals home to bring color to your cooking.

▮ 2312 N. Lincoln Ave. (bet. Belden Ave. & Childrens Plz.)
▮ Fullerton
✆ (773) 697-4750 — **WEB:** www.rickshawrepublic.com
▮ Dinner Tue – Sun   **PRICE:** ⊚⊚

SUMMER HOUSE SANTA MONICA ¶O

American

✕✕ | 🍸 🦽 ☂ 🛋 🖐

MAP: D4

Sunny days and southern California come to Lincoln Park in the form of this bright and breezy restaurant that resembles a beach house, albeit an enormous one with lots of house guests. It's the perfect choice for a summer's day—and not a bad one in the colder months either, if you're having a quick bite before the theater or want to shake off those winter blues for a while. There's even a countdown showing the number of days till summer.

The menu proves a good fit for the surroundings by keeping things easy. There are sandwiches, tacos, and salads, but it's the meat and fish from the wood-fired oven that stand out. For dessert, choose a big cookie from the counter by the entrance. There's also a pizza restaurant and bar attached.

▦ 1954 N. Halsted St. (bet. Armitage Ave. & Willow St.)
🚇 Armitage
✆ (773) 634-4100 — **WEB:** www.summerhousesm.com
▦ Lunch & dinner daily   **PRICE:** $$

TWIN ANCHORS ¶O

Barbecue

✕ | 🍺 ☂ 🖐

MAP: E4

Within the brick walls that have housed Twin Anchors since 1932, generations have made their way across the checkerboard linoleum floor to throw a quarter in the jukebox and get saucy with a slab of their legendary ribs in one of the curved booths. Though the bar is wall-to-wall on weekends, most weekdays are low-key, with families and groups ready for a casual night out.

Fall-off-the-bone baby back ribs are the real deal, made with a sweet and spicy rub, served with their own "zesty" sauce or the newer Prohibition version, with brown sugar and a wallop of ghost-pepper heat. Classic sides like onion rings, baked beans, or hearty chili round out the meal. If there's a wait at this no-reservations spot, try the beer of the month while cooling your heels.

▦ 1655 N. Sedgwick St. (at Eugenie St.)
🚇 Sedgwick
✆ (312) 266-1616 — **WEB:** www.twinanchorsribs.com
▦ Lunch Sat - Sun   Dinner nightly   **PRICE:** $$

LOOP
& STREETERVILLE

The relentless pace and race of Chicago's main business district is named after the "El" tracks that make a "loop" around the area. Their cacophony may be an intrinsic part of the city's soundtrack, but this neighborhood has always had a culinary resonance as well. In fact, it is one that is perpetually evolving. It wasn't that long ago that the Loop turned into no-man's land once the business crowd headed home for the night. However thanks to a revitalized Theater District, new residential high-rises, sleek hotels and student dorms, the tumbleweeds have been replaced with a buoyant dining scene, wine boutiques, and gourmet stores that stay open well past dusk. Start your culinary pilgrimage by exploring **Block 37**, one of the city's original 58 blocks. It took decades of hard work and several political dynasties, but the block now houses a five-story atrium with shopping, restaurants, and access to public transport. Next up: **Tesori**, a buzzing trattoria serving hand-crafted pastas to a set of suits. Top off these savory bites with a dash of sweet at the Chicago outpost of NYC hot spot, **Magnolia Bakery**. Get in line here for goodies like cupcakes and banana pudding. For those watching their waistline, probiotic **Lifeway Kefir Shop**—with delicious frozen yogurts—is heaven on earth. And, catering to the clusters of corporate types in the area are several fast-casual options on the Pedway level (a system of tunnels that links crucial downtown buildings underground— also a godsend during those brutal Chicago winters.) For a quick grab-and-go lunch, **Hannah's Bretzel** is ace. Revered as "über sandwich makers," their version of the namesake, crafted from freshly baked German bread, features unique fillings (imagine a grass-fed sirloin sammie spread with nutty Gruyère, vine tomatoes, and horseradish aïoli). While summer brings a mélange of musical acts to Millennium Park, Grant Park, and the Petrillo Music Shell that are just begging for a picnic,

winter evenings are best spent at **The Walnut Room**. Besides people-watching, a family-friendly vibe, and stunning Christmas décor, this Macy's gem also warms the soul with comfort food like Mrs. Hering's Chicken Pot Pie—the recipe for which dates back to 1890. Food enthusiasts also flock to **Park Grill**, a full-service restaurant, flanked by an ice rink in the winter. Of course, no trip to the Windy City, much less the Loop, would be complete without tasting the Italian specialties from **Vivere**—a beloved local institution that seamlessly blends formality with spirited charm in a handsome space.

TOURING & CAROUSING

Calling all sweet tooths: with flavors like maple-bacon and pistachio-Meyer lemon, you will be hard-pressed to stop at just one doughnut variety at **Do-Rite**. But, if dessert doesn't do it for you, eat your way through the city by way of **Tastebud Tours'** Loop route, whose stops may include **The Berghoff**— one of the oldest known

restaurants in town, with an impressive bar pouring steins of beer. Equally popular is the **Chicago Pizza Tour**, also headquartered here. From visiting restaurant kitchens, getting schooled on top ingredients, brick ovens, the physics of pizza-making, and digging into deep-dish pies (naturally!), this expedition is designed to showcase the true essence behind the city's most iconic (deep) dish. During warmer months, several farmer's markets cater to the downtown crowd. These may even include the ones stationed at Federal Plaza on Tuesdays or Daley Plaza on Thursdays. Though concession carts continue to dot the streets in nearby Millennium Park, home cooks are in for a serious treat at **Mariano's**. This gourmet emporium proffers everything from gluten-free lemon bars for stiletto-clad socialites to holiday gifts for area businesses. **Printers Row Wine Shop's** carefully curated wine selection and weekly wine tastings (every Friday at 5:00 P.M.) make it the district's go-to wine stop—intent on equipping real folks with the right amount of information. Chicago, however, also sees its fair share of coffee connoisseurs, and tourists tired of sightseeing should be sure to stop in for a pick-me-up at **Intelligentsia Coffee**—a local chain with an emphasis on direct trade. Locations can be found all over, but the **Millennium Park Coffeebar** is especially convenient and delicious.

One of the Windy City's biggest events (and the second largest attraction in the state of Illinois) is **Taste of Chicago**—a five-day summer extravaganza in Grant Park. For the last 30 years, the festival's never-ending maze of real food booths and live music has attracted hordes of hungry diners from all over. It may be hot and crowded, but that's just part of the fun... for some!

STREETERVILLE

Bound by the strategically set Chicago River, swanky Magnificent Mile and sparkling Lake Michigan, Streeterville is a precious locality, housing hotels and high-rises alongside offices, universities, and museums. If that doesn't boast cultural diversity, the sights and smells at Water Tower Place's **Foodlife** offer indisputable proof. Located on the mezzanine floor of the shopping mall, this simple food court has been elevated to an art form. A veritable "United Nations of food courts," Foodlife draws a devoted following to its 14 different kitchens that may whip up everything from Chinese potstickers and deep-dish pizza to crunchy fried chicken. Unlike other food courts, you're given a card that can be swiped at as many stalls as you choose. Once you've had your fill, bring the card to the cash register to receive your balance, and *voila*, there's just a single bill to pay! Another notable tenant of Water Tower Place is **Wow Bao** that doles out some of the best steamed veggie- and meat-filled buns around. In fact, they were so popular that four locations sprouted downtown. Hopping skyscrapers, the famous **John Hancock Center** is known to many as a "food lover's paradise." Here, bachelors in business suits come to shop for groceries with sky-high prices to match the staggering view at **Potash Brothers** (open to residents only). But for those whose tastes run

more toward champagne and cocktails than cheeseburgers with crinkle-cut fries, there's always the **Signature Room**, located on the 96th floor. A sensational setting for quenching nightcaps, this dining room also presents an incredible brunch, lunch, dinner, and dessert menu, all of which employ some of the finest ingredients in town. While their creative cocktails may result in sticker shock, the twinkling cityscape will have you...at hello. From high-rise sips to street-level spreads, find a score of lucky locals dining with fine wine at **Volare Ristorante Italiano**.

ART & CULTURE

The Museum of Contemporary Art is located next to Lake Shore Park, an outdoor recreational extravaganza. Well-known for housing the world's leading collection of modern art, patrons who come here know to balance the gravitas of this setting with fresh nourishment from their in-house restaurant. But, it's also the peppers and potatoes that lure foodies to the farmer's market, held at

the museum every Tuesday from June through October. Choose to bookend a home-cooked meal with some dark chocolate from **Godiva**—a beautiful boutique carrying it all, from chocolate-covered strawberries and truffles to gourmet biscuits, snacks, and bars. The world convenes at Chicago's lakefront **Navy Pier** for a day of exploration and eats. Showcasing lush gardens and parks in conjunction with shops and dining stalls, families usually flock to **Bubba Gump Shrimp Co.** for its convivial vibe and shrimp specials. But, locals looking for live music with their carnitas and margaritas may head to **Jimmy Buffett's Margaritaville Bar & Grill** (named after the rockstar himself). For nibbling in between meals, venture towards **Garrett Popcorn Shops**, which promises to have you hooked on sweet-and-salty flavors like CheeseCorn and Macadamia CaramelCrisp. The choices are plenty and you can even create your own tin here. Then move on to more substantial meals that may include an all-natural Chicago-style dog (slathered with mustard, onion, relish, sport peppers, tomatoes, and celery salt) from **America's Dog**. This classic destination showcases an impressive range of city-style creations from Houston, New York, and Philadelphia, to Detroit, Kansas City, and San Francisco. Of course, meat-lovers who mean business never miss **M Burger**, always buzzing with business lunchers, tourists, and shoppers alike. In fact, it should be renamed "mmm" burger simply for its juicy parcels of bacon, cheese, and secret sauce. Even calorie counters may rest easy as the "fowl mouth burger," a spicy barbecue turkey version is nothing less than divine. For a bit more intimacy and lot more fantasy, **Sayat Nova** is superb. Highlighting a menu of kibbee alongside more exotic signatures like sarma or meat- and veggie-filled grape leaves bobbing in a light garlic sauce, this Middle Eastern marvel keeps its options limited but fan-base infinite.

Residents know that Chicago is big on breakfast—so big that they can even have it for dinner—maybe at Michigan Avenue's **West Egg**. This convivial café-cum-coffee corridor serves three square meals a day, but it is their breakfast specials (choose between pancakes, waffles, or other "eggcellent" dishes) that keep the joint jumping at all times. Finally, the Northwestern Memorial Hospital complex is another esteemed establishment that dominates the local landscape. Besides its top medical services, a parade of dining gems (think coffee shops plus ethnic food eateries) catering to their staff and students, visitors loom large over this neighborhood—and lake.

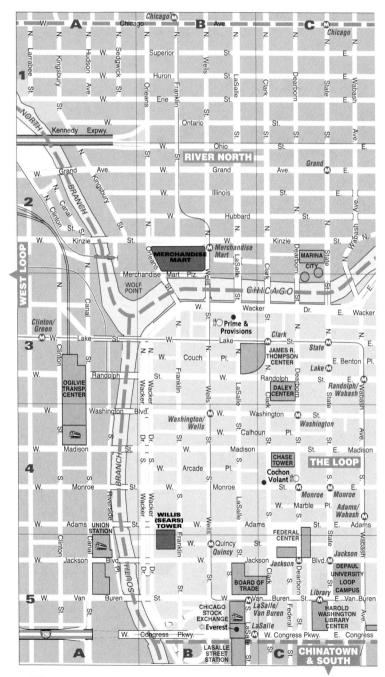

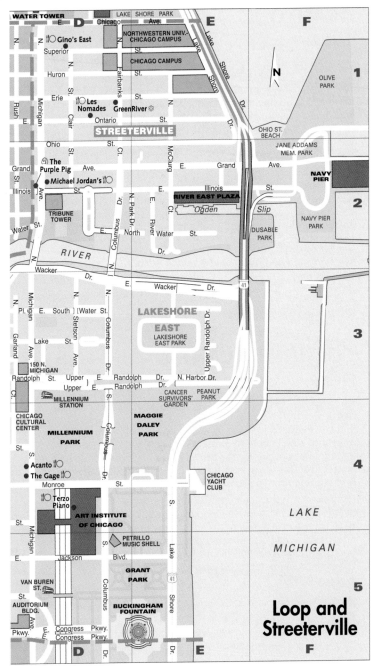

WATER TOWER

LAKE SHORE PARK

Gino's East

NORTHWESTERN UNIV. CHICAGO CAMPUS

CHICAGO CAMPUS

N

1

OLIVE PARK

Superior

Huron

Erie

Les Nomades

GreenRiver

STREETERVILLE

Ontario

OHIO ST. BEACH

JANE ADDAMS MEM. PARK

Ohio

The Purple Pig

Grand

Michael Jordan's

Illinois

TRIBUNE TOWER

Grand

Illinois

RIVER EAST PLAZA

Ogden

Slip

DUSABLE PARK

NAVY PIER

NAVY PIER PARK

Water

North

Water

RIVER

Wacker

Wacker

41

LAKESHORE

EAST

LAKESHORE EAST PARK

2

3

Lake

150 N. MICHIGAN

Randolph

Upper

Randolph

Upper

Randolph

N. Harbor Dr.

CANCER SURVIVORS' GARDEN

PEANUT PARK

MILLENNIUM STATION

CHICAGO CULTURAL CENTER

MILLENNIUM PARK

MAGGIE DALEY PARK

Acanto

The Gage

Monroe

CHICAGO YACHT CLUB

4

Terzo Piano

ART INSTITUTE OF CHICAGO

PETRILLO MUSIC SHELL

Jackson

Blvd.

GRANT PARK

41

LAKE

MICHIGAN

VAN BUREN ST.

AUDITORIUM BLDG.

Congress Pkwy.

Congress Pkwy.

BUCKINGHAM FOUNTAIN

5

Loop and Streeterville

ACANTO ¶O
Italian

XX | 器 🍹 🎣   **MAP:** D4

This Italian reincarnation set in the former Henri space knows how to make an impression: its prime location across from Millennium Park would be a looker any day, but it goes the extra mile with style and sociability. The dining room is striking with angular light fixtures and orange banquettes; a luminous marble bar and matching tables lend a masculine, sophisticated vibe.

The carte's Italian standards are amped up to luxurious levels, like the Treviso and white bean salad with fennel, golden raisins, and crispy pancetta; or house-made duck egg spaghetti drenched in a cream sauce and twirled around rapini, spicy pork sausage, and caramelized onions. For dessert, a fresh ricotta tart is highlighted by bittersweet orange marmalade.

▪ 18 S. Michigan Ave. (bet. Madison & Monroe Sts.)
🚇 Monroe
✆ (312) 578-0763 — **WEB:** www.acantochicago.com
▪ Lunch & dinner daily   PRICE: $$

COCHON VOLANT ¶O
French

XX | 🍹 ⴺ 🏠 🚅 🎣   **MAP:** C4

Though it's attached to the Hyatt, Cochon Volant is quickly becoming a favorite with Loop and Streterville locals and sightseers alike for its timeless warmth. Round bistro tables and bentwood chairs are clustered across the mosaic-tiled floor, while a broad, marble-topped bar is bustling with patrons from lunch to happy hour.

Brasserie favorites dominate the menu, ranging from rustic French onion soup to lavish raw seafood plateaux. Steak frites are juicy and flavorsome with a tender prime cut of bavette, offered with five sauce options like a classic béarnaise or rich Roquefort. Breakfast is delicious, but for those who don't have time to sit and stay a while, the takeaway bakery lets commuters snag a pastry and coffee to go.

▪ 100 W. Monroe St. (at Clark St.)
🚇 Monroe
✆ (312) 754-6560 — **WEB:** www.cochonvolantchicago.com
▪ Lunch & dinner daily   PRICE: $$

EVEREST ✤

French

XxX | 🕸 🔥 ⬜ 🍳

Summit the historic Chicago Stock Exchange building via a private elevator to reach the sophisticated—though never outdated—scene at Everest on the 40th floor. The sunken-level dining room stays dimly lit by contemporary circular metal light fixtures, all the better to gaze admiringly at the views from the windows framing the formal space. Heavy white linens and abstract bronze sculptures adorn each table, at which smartly dressed guests take it all in.

Alsatian Chef Jean Joho keeps to French tradition on his degustation and prix-fixe menus, with nods to local ingredients among the classical techniques and pairings presented nightly. Where other chefs may feel the need to update and tweak time-honored dishes, Everest celebrates the classics. Subtle hints of ginger in a rich Gewürztraminer butter sauce complement succulent chunks of fresh Maine lobster. Two thick, bone-in lamb chops, ringed elegantly with flavorful fat, are toothsome but not too chewy—their richness amplified by a delicate, silken spring garlic flan and a bed of crisp green beans that soak up the thyme jus.

Cap it all off with tart and sweet pistachio vanilla succès dabbed with red rhubarb jam.

◾ 440 S. LaSalle St. (bet. Congress Pkwy. & Van Buren St.)
🚇 LaSalle/Van Buren
📞 (312) 663-8920 — **WEB:** www.everestrestaurant.com
◾ Dinner Tue – Sat   PRICE: $$$$

THE GAGE 🍴

Gastropub

✕✕ | 🍺 ♿ 🪑 🖼 🛋 ✒

MAP: D4

For 10 years, this expansive, eclectic gastropub has catered to the Millennium Park crowds. Handsome banquettes and columns wrapped in celadon tiles lend a clubby allure, but the space's buzzy vibe never feels overwhelming. While a bar stretching half the length of the restaurant gets its fair share of happy-hour crowds, the rear dining rooms offer a more relaxed setting.

Pub classics with flair define the menu, like malt-battered cod with creamy tartar sauce and parsley-flecked thick-cut fries—a solid rendition of fish and chips. Keep it light with crunchy watercress and sugar snap pea salad with house-made burrata, or go all out with a plate of chocolate-toffee cream puffs garnished with tender cocoa-dusted marshmallows.

🔲 24 S. Michigan Ave. (bet. Madison & Monroe Sts.)
🚇 Madison
📞 (312) 372-4243 — **WEB:** www.thegagechicago.com
🔲 Lunch & dinner daily

PRICE: $$

GINO'S EAST 🍴

Pizza

✕ | ♿ 🖼 ✒

MAP: D1

Pizza pilgrims continue to make the trek to the original location of this renowned local deep-dish chain, where a 45-minute wait is the norm. However, solo diners may rest easy as they can order personal pies from a walk-up counter. The walls, scribbled with years of graffiti, are nearly as iconic as the high-walled pies themselves, whose crusts get their signature crunch from cornmeal and searing-hot metal pans with two inch-high sides.

Filled with heaps of mozzarella and toppings like the "Meaty Legend" lineup of spicy pepperoni, Italian sausage, and both Canadian and regular bacon before getting sauced, it's hard for some to eat more than two wedges here. Nonconformists can of course opt for thin-crust pies, gussied up by add-ons like roasted red peppers.

🔲 162 E. Superior St. (bet. Michigan Ave. & St. Clair St.)
🚇 Chicago (Red)
📞 (312) 266-3337 — **WEB:** www.ginoseast.com
🔲 Lunch & dinner daily

PRICE: $$

GREENRIVER ✿

American

✗✗ | 🍸 ♿ 🛋 🏠 🛋 🤚

When a cocktail carte is arranged by base ingredient (corn, rye, agave) rather than the spirits made from them, a serious focus on drinking is immediately clear—and we should expect no less from the mixology gurus behind New York City's The Dead Rabbit. Your cocktails, wines, and green cardamom sodas are going to be masterpieces, yet the cuisine is anything but an afterthought.

Whether you make it to a table or just end up staying at the bar, be sure to order some of the city's most luscious beef tartare, topped with shaved horseradish, quail egg yolk, and judiciously dressed with capers, anchovies, and onion. If you prefer your meat perfectly cooked, try the Slagel Farm ribeye, carved tableside and set in a pool of rich bone marrow jus and draped atop cipollini, mushrooms and a potato purée. Desserts are refreshing and none-too-sweet, like the wintery citrus chiboust garnished with sugared cranberries, fennel fronds, and red-veined sorrel leaves—surrounded by a nest of crisp-baked pastry threads.

And even though lunch may seem corporate, the 18th-floor location commands panoramic views of the city and is ideal at all times of day. In fine weather, the wraparound terrace is unbeatable.

◾ 259 E. Erie St., 18th fl. (at Fairbanks Ct.)
🚇 Grand (Red)
✆ (312) 337-0101 — **WEB:** www.greenriverchi.com
◾ Lunch daily   Dinner Mon – Sat   **PRICE:** $$$

LES NOMADES 🍴

French

XxX | 🕸 🖐️

MAP: D1

A giddy excitement bubbles through the air at Les Nomades, and with good reason: this intimate, charming restaurant feels like a secret hideaway within a gated Streeterville brownstone. Owner Mary Beth Liccioni welcomes all as if they were old friends, seating guests among the graciously arranged fresh flowers, framed artwork, and linen-topped tables.

Though the fragrant herb-loaded lavash presented at each table is good enough to make an entire meal out of, save room for entrées like grilled Scottish salmon, served medium-rare with a colorful, flavorful blend of beets, cucumber, and black olive tapenade. A single translucent langoustine raviolo duets on a plate with tempura soft shell crab, both enhanced by harissa- and saffron-spiked rouille.

▪ 222 E. Ontario St. (bet. Fairbanks Ct. & St. Clair St.)
▪ Grand (Red)
✆ (312) 649-9010 — **WEB:** www.lesnomades.net
▪ Dinner Tue – Sat

PRICE: $$$$

MICHAEL JORDAN'S 🍴

Steakhouse

XxX | 🕸 ♿ 🖵 🖐️

MAP: D2

Leave your dated 1993 Bulls jersey in the closet for a meal at this swanky steakhouse, tucked just off the lobby of the InterContinental Hotel. Leather and velvet accents telegraph an upscale vibe, and references to His Airness are subtle—from oversized sepia photographs of basketball netting to a 23-layer chocolate cake for dessert.

A glass of Amarone with a dry-aged Porterhouse is always a slam-dunk, but the kitchen also turns out pleasing modern twists on steakhouse classics. Chicago's famous Italian beef gets an upgrade with smoked ribeye and aged provolone. Similarly, the traditional wedge salad is presented as a halved small head of baby romaine, layered here with creamy Wisconsin blue cheese and thick slabs of crispy bacon.

▪ 505 N. Michigan Ave. (bet. Grand Ave. & Illinois St.)
▪ Grand (Red)
✆ (312) 321-8823 — **WEB:** www.mjshchicago.com
▪ Lunch & dinner daily

PRICE: $$$

PRIME & PROVISIONS 🍴

Steakhouse

XxX | 🐝 ♿ 🏕 ⎵   **MAP:** B3

Though it would also feel at home in Las Vegas, this glitzy oversized steakhouse fits right in with its swanky Chicago riverfront neighbors. The polished, masculine interior makes its priorities clear from the get-go, showcasing a two-story wine tower and a peek into the dry-aging room under bold, barrel-vaulted ceilings and chandeliers.

A starter of chewy rosemary-sea salt monkey bread whets the palate, while rosy pink slices of slow-roasted bone-in prime rib, rubbed with a crust of fragrant herbs, take a classic hoagie to new heights. When paired with house-cut fries and creamy horseradish dip, it's a meal to rival a Porterhouse. But save room for dessert: a single-serving banana cream pie with loads of whipped cream is a whimsical final bite.

🔲 222 N. LaSalle St. (at Wacker Dr.)
🚇 Clark/Lake
📞 (312) 726-7777 — **WEB:** www.primeandprovisions.com
🔲 Lunch Mon – Fri Dinner Mon – Sat   **PRICE:** $$$

THE PURPLE PIG 😀

Mediterranean

X | 🐝 🏕   **MAP:** D2

No matter the time of day, this is a fave among groups craving first-rate Mediterranean cooking with drinks and a setting to match. Everything is tasty, fun, and great for sharing, so go with a posse and get a communal table all to yourselves. The bar is just as nice for solo dining, thanks to the chatty staff.

The menu covers a range of specialties from the Med, from panini to a la plancha. But, don't miss starting with the incredibly smart take on cannolo filled with whipped burrata, mixed with candied, puréed and ground pistachios, as well as a minty herb salsa and butternut squash. Also try tender and nicely charred octopus with green beans, fingerling potatoes, and salsa verde. Finally, delve into their selection of top-notch cheese and charcuterie.

🔲 500 N. Michigan Ave. (at Illinois St.)
🚇 Grand (Red)
📞 (312) 464-1744 — **WEB:** www.thepurplepigchicago.com
🔲 Lunch & dinner daily   **PRICE:** $$

TERZO PIANO ⓘ○

Italian

XX | ♿ 🏠 🏕 ⚟ **MAP:** D4

Whether you're taking in the modern masterpieces at The Art Institute or simply enjoying lunch and cocktails on the sculpture-filled garden terrace, Terzo Piano is a feast for all the senses. The windowed room is mod and minimalist, allowing the artistry of the Mediterranean-influenced menu to shine brightly at each table.

With Tony Mantuano overseeing the kitchen, Italian influences find their way into many seasonal dishes. Charred tomato crème fraîche lends luxurious smokiness and a tart streak to tender chicken Milanese resting on roasted cipollini purée. And agnolotti bursting with a sweet pea-ricotta filling find savory balance with shards of crispy pancetta.

As an added bonus, museum members receive a 10 percent discount on the meal.

▨ 159 E. Monroe St. (in the Art Institute of Chicago)
🚇 Monroe
✆ (312) 443-8650 — **WEB:** www.terzopianochicago.com
▨ Lunch daily Dinner Thu **PRICE:** $$

Remember, stars ✿
are awarded for cuisine only! Elements
such as service and décor are not a factor.

PILSEN, UNIVERSITY VILLAGE & BRIDGEPORT

This cluster of neighborhoods packs a perfect punch, both in terms of food and sheer vitality. It lives up to every expectation and reputation, so get ready for a tour packed with literal, acoustic, and visual flavor. The Little Italy moniker applies to a stretch of Taylor Street that abuts the University (of Illinois at Chicago) Village neighborhood, and it's bigger and more authentically Italian than it first appears. The streets are as stuffed with epicurean shops as an Italian beef is with meat. So, bring an appetite and try this iconic (and messy) Chicago specialty at **Al's No. 1 Italian Beef**. After combing through the supply at **Conte Di Savoia**, an Italian grocery and takeout spot, stop for lunch at **Fontano's Subs** (locally famous for their hearty subs) or old-school **Bacchanalia**.

Brunch your way through the day at **Pleasant House Bakery**; then save room for creative tamales (think roasted pepper-goat cheese) at **Dia De Los Tamales**, a great little spot replete with a funky décor. Speaking of south-of-the-border fun, don't miss out on the much-loved festival, **Mole de Mayo**, featuring an enticing lineup of Mexican cuisine mingled with cultural events. Parched after a long day on your feet? **Mario's Italian Lemonade** is where you can seal the deal over a frozen fruit slush. Later, consider popping into **Scafuri Bakery** for a sugar refill, some biscotti, or *sfogliatelle*. This charming retreat has been delivering

traditional Italian sweets to the community since opening its doors in 1904. Popular for fresh-baked breads, pastries, and cookies, wedding cakes and pies are also part of their ever-changing repertoire.

UNIVERSITY VILLAGE

Like any self-respecting college "town," University Village is home to a range of toasty coffee shops. Add to that the mélange of doctors, medical students, nurses, and others working in the neighborhood hospital, and you've got a perpetually bustling vibe with great people-watching potential. Take a break from the hustle to quench your thirst at one among a few select locations

of **Lush Wine & Spirits**. On Sundays, follow the band of locals to **Maxwell Street Market**. Having relocated to Desplaines Street in 2008, this sprawling bazaar welcomes over 500 vendors selling fresh produce, amazing Mexican eats, and other miscellanea. Then watch celebrity chef, Rick Bayless, as he peruses these stalls for dried chilies or epazote, while lesser Gods can be seen gorging on tacos and tostadas.

PILSEN & BRIDGEPORT

Chicagoland's massive Mexican population (more than 650,000 according to the latest U.S. Census count) has built a patchwork of regional specialties, many of which are found in the south side's residential Pilsen and Little Village neighborhoods. Pilsen is also home to the free National Museum of Mexican Art, the only Latino museum accredited by the American Alliance of Museums, as well as countless taquerias and bakeries. **Birrieria Reyes de Ocotlan** is an authentic find for tender, delicious, and flavorful goat meat

folded into juicy tacos. If that sounds too gamey, then **Pollo Express** oozing with the tantalizing aroma of whole char-grilled chicken, is always reliable. Join their endless line for Styrofoam containers filled with creamy guacamole, adobo-rubbed chicken, and sweet empanadas. Everyone goes all out for Mexican Independence Day in September including area restaurants, while the Little Village Arts Festival packs 'em in each fall. Just as the **Pilsen Community Market** held every Sunday in the Chicago Community Bank, with its assortment of fruits and vegetables, does much to replenish the soul, carb addicts get their fix at **Sabinas Food Products**. And for a Mexican-themed evening at home, **La Casa del Pueblo** is an exceptional supermarket that offers all things imaginable, including household, health, and beauty essentials. On the other hand, carnivores continue to gush over **Carnitas Uruapan's** pork carnitas paired with salty *chicharrónes*. Since 1950, **Taqueria El Milagro** has been proffering a unique taste with its cafeteria-style restaurant complete with a tamale-centric menu, as well as a store bursting with burritos and tortillas. But, lovers of all things "green" can't resist the siren call of **Simone's Bar**. This eco-friendly joint is hip and heavenly for a variety of sips. And over in Bridgeport, **Maria's Packaged Goods & Community Bar** has been a neighborhood institution in one form or another since 1939. Here, antique collectible beer cans line the space, and leftover beer bottle clusters are being constantly repurposed as chandeliers.

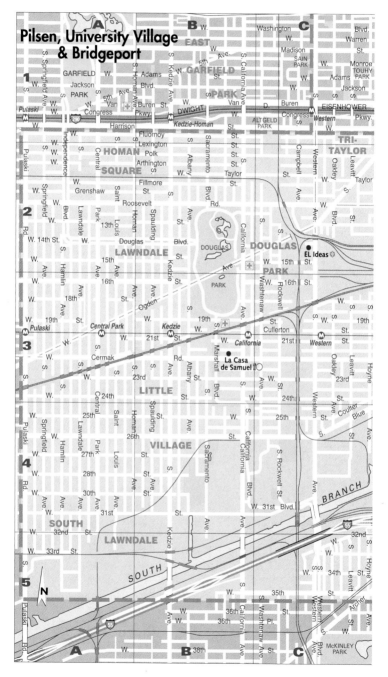

Pilsen, University Village & Bridgeport

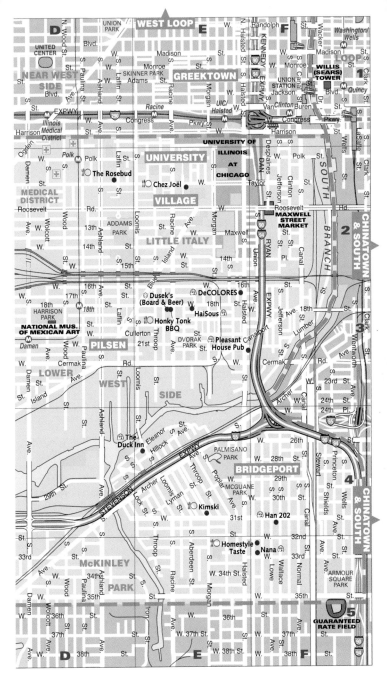

CHEZ JOËL 🍴

French

✕✕ | 🍸 🏠 🛋 🧺   **MAP:** E2

Bringing a bit of je ne sais quoi to Little Italy, Chez Joël is a stylish setting packed with expats and locals recalling their travel stories. Here, walls gleam with ice-blue accents, windows are dressed with velvet, and art that is nothing less than ace adds to the overall lure. A cozy bar in the back is ideal for sipping, but then get down to business by partaking in this kitchen's cuisine—classic French mingled with global effects.

For a pleasing trio of flavors, cuisses de grenouilles à la Provençale, or frogs legs, are cooked with garlic, spinach and just the right dab of butter, just as poulet aux champignons, or chicken breast, is sautéed in a white wine- mushroom- and cream-sauce. Classic desserts round out the menu, but crème brûlée is not a bad way to go.

🔲 1119 W. Taylor St. (bet. Aberdeen & May Sts.)
☎ (312) 226-6479 — **WEB:** www.chezjoelbistro.com
🔲 Lunch Tue – Sat Dinner Tue – Sun   **PRICE: $$**

DECOLORES 😊

Mexican

✕✕ | ♿ 🏠 📺 🛋   **MAP:** E3

This Mexican restaurant's slate-colored walls feature a beautiful rotation of work from local artists, making the walls a great conversation starter even before the delicious fare hits your table. The lovely bar is yet another bit of artistry, featuring shelves tucked around a series of metal branches; and a wonderful, colorful flower motif on the back wall. A relaxed atmosphere, warm service staff and well-made cocktails seal the deal.

At this kitchen, many of the recipes have been passed down through the family for generations—and one taste of the silky mole poblano, laced over chicken and served with excellent refried beans and yellow rice, will transport you back to the motherland. Round out dinner with a wickedly good homemade cheesecake flan.

🔲 1626 S. Halsted St. (bet. 16th & 17th Sts.)
☎ (312) 226-9886 — **WEB:** www.decolor.us
🔲 Lunch Sat – Sun Dinner Tue – Sun   **PRICE: $$**

THE DUCK INN 😷

Gastropub

XX | 🍸 🍺 ♿ 🏛 🛋

Head to the Bridgeport warehouses, where this stylish, modern tavern—helmed by Executive Chef Kris Delee—feels like a diamond in the rough. Then make your way past the buzzy bar (pouring heady cocktails) to a semi-open kitchen, which is in full view of the decorous dining room featuring wood tables and mid-century seats.

The cuisine may be coined as "working-class fine dining," but there is nothing lowbrow about this menu, which unveils a focused but diverse selection of small plates and mains. Japanese barbecue sauce and sesame seeds are the crowning touch to duck wings, while foie gras mousse with celery fronds and brioche is a study in fine flavors and textures. Of course, regulars know to save room for the glistening Alaskan halibut with rye crumbs.

◻ 2701 S. Eleanor St. (at Loomis St.)
℘ (312) 724-8811 — **WEB:** www.theduckinnchicago.com
◻ Lunch Sat – Sun   Dinner Tue – Sun   PRICE: $$

HAISOUS 😷

Vietnamese

XX | ♿ 🖥 🛋 📱

The passion project of Chef Thai Dang and his wife, Danielle, HaiSous offers refined Vietnamese cuisine in a plum, gorgeous setting. The menu is divided into five sections, and it's filled with some wonderful, lesser-known (and possibly unexpected) compositions you won't want to miss.

The restaurant offers an array of seating options: an open kitchen, fringed with comfy round seats; a bar area for cocktails and perhaps an order of those famous chicken wings; as well as two dining rooms, one fitted out with communal seating. Don't leave without sampling the refreshing goi vit (duck salad); cánh gà chiên (chicken wings, fragrant with fish sauce, garlic and chili); or tender eggplant and octopus, laced with coconut cream and crispy fried shallots.

◻ 1800 S. Carpenter Ave. (at 18th St.)
🚇 18th
℘ (312) 702-1303 — **WEB:** www.haisous.com
◻ Lunch Sat – Sun   Dinner Mon – Sat   PRICE: $$

CHICAGO ▶ PILSEN, UNIVERSITY VILLAGE & BRIDGEPORT

DUSEK'S (BOARD & BEER) ✿

Gastropub

✕✕ | 🍺 ♿ 🛷

On the one hand, Dusek's is simply a great gastropub, serving food that is as tasty and down-to earth as one of their wood fire-roasted pretzels, tucked with gooey cheese and wickedly hot beer mustard. On the other hand, this is just the place to meet friends or grab a bite before heading to a concert at Thalia Music Hall, located next door.

The fact that this spot is named for the man who founded the original venue back in 1892 shows the importance of this connection—those in-the-know are usually headed here before or after a show. The space seems dark and moody, but everyone is having a rollicking good time. The front room feels more like a tavern; the back is a dining room warmed by the wood-burning ovens. Yet both share that same friendly ambience and superb service.

Menu pleasers include goat cheese "ravioli" set over a purée of oven-roasted red peppers and sweet corn, finished with crushed hazelnuts and basil oil; as well as zaruela, featuring seafood broth-infused bomba rice topped with Atlantic cod, Manila clams and Gulf prawns. A splash of preserved lemon enriches this beautiful composition, not unlike the fresh blueberries that star alongside a rich and buttery chocolate-pecan tart.

🔲 1227 W. 18th St. (at Allport St.)
🚇 18th
📞 (312) 526-3851 — **WEB:** www.dusekschicago.com
🔲 Lunch & dinner daily

PRICE: $$

EL IDEAS ❀
Contemporary

XX | BYO

MAP: C2

Dining here feels like attending an underground dinner party prepared by a merry band of misfit cooks in Chef Phillip Foss' home (he lives right upstairs). There is one seating, everyone is served at the same time, and meals are prepaid so guests can linger or leave at their leisure. The fact that the restaurant resembles a test kitchen is heightened when guests are told to manage their BYO beverages themselves and cooks deliver dishes to your table. Don't worry—they turn the music down so you can hear each description. Yet this is all part of the show; it's a fun, friendly, totally unique experience.

The cuisine follows suit and works wonders by pushing—if not completely disregarding—the traditional boundaries of cooking. Outlandish surprises begin with tosaka (Japanese seaweed) accompanied by chopped raw scallop topped with creamy scrambled eggs, Ghost pepper-infused caviar, and shaved air-dried tuna. A humble sounding "ham and cheese" is actually intensely savory jamón Ibérico beneath a dome of fragrant black truffles and cheese fonduta over house-made potato bread.

Finish with a bowl of playful nostalgia that tastes better than childhood: chocolate cake batter with spatulas for licking it up.

🔲 2419 W. 14th St. (at Western Ave.)
🚇 Western (Pink)
✆ (312) 226-8144 — **WEB:** www.elideas.com
🔲 Dinner Tue – Sat

PRICE: $$$$

HAN 202 ☺

Asian

XX | ♿ BYO   **MAP:** F4

Near U.S. Cellular Field, this is the perfect spot to stop for an early meal before a White Sox game. The dining room feels polished and sophisticated, with leather-backed seats, large windows, and contemporary artwork.

The menu follows suit with food that is also an elegant departure from expectation, with cooking that is more Asian than specifically Chinese. The prix-fixe menu supplements may only be a few dollars more, but are well worth it. Diver scallops are wildly pristine and delicious, pan-seared and served with red beet and smoked yellow pepper purées over white chocolate sabayon jus. The plump bone-in rack of lamb is wonderful, as is its bonito plum sauce deeply flavored with lavender, mustard seeds, and Sichuan pepper.

◼ 605 W. 31st St. (bet. Lowe Ave. & Wallace St.)
✆ (312) 949-1314 — **WEB:** www.han202.com
◼ Dinner Tue – Sun   **PRICE: $$**

HOMESTYLE TASTE ⊘

Chinese

X | ♿ BYO   **MAP:** F5

For even more adventurous fare than spicy Sichuan lamb or dim sum, look no further than this family-run favorite. Though the lengthy menu offers plenty of usual suspects (think scallion pancakes and mapo tofu), it's also chock-full of Chinese dishes that will make any offal lover's day.

Thin slices of lamb kidney are dry stir-fried, their mild flavor boosted by copious amounts of cumin and red chilies. Then, a sweet and sour sauce offsets the funky flavor of quick-fried intestine, tripe, and liver; and pickled cabbage and pork meatball soup, boosted by tofu and noodles, is a welcome warmer on cold days. The service is friendly and amenable, so don't be afraid to specify your preferred meat or ask for chili oil to amplify the heat quotient.

◼ 3205 S. Halsted St. (bet. 32nd & 33rd Sts.)
✆ (312) 949-9328 — **WEB:** N/A
◼ Lunch & dinner daily   **PRICE: ⊖**

HONKY TONK BBQ 🍴

Barbecue

✗

A rousing success since it opened in 2007, Honky Tonk BBQ serves up live music and award-winning Memphis-style treats on the southwest side of the city. Though the rollicking bar up front takes its cues from a swinging Wild West saloon, the rear dining room offers a more sedate—though still eclectic—setting for sipping house cocktails and chowing down on sensational smoked meats.

You'll need two hands to hold homemade empanadas stuffed with combinations like Manchego cheese and shiitake mushrooms, and extra cottony white bread to soak up the juices of bone-in, wood-smoked chicken. Brisket chili is even more robust with a scoop of creamy mac and cheese. And if you're still hungry, soda floats with Bridgeport-made Filbert's root beer are the cherry on top.

■ 1800 S. Racine Ave. (at 18th St.)

🚇 18th

✆ (312) 226-7427 — **WEB:** www.honkytonkbbqchicago.com

■ Dinner Tue – Sun   **PRICE:** $$

KIMSKI 🍴

Fusion

✗ | 🍺 ♿ 🏠 ✍

This long-awaited development in Bridgeport, connected to the popular Maria's Packaged Goods & Community Bar, serves up deliciousness and fun in equal parts. Think quirky Korean-Polish fusion menu; daily mish-mash specials; and T-shirts as well as fireball sauces to take home. All the food can be ordered at the counter to-go, but do yourself a favor and make your way to the open industrial dining space or large patio to enjoy the jamming bar and some live music with your food.

Everything at Kimski is truly unique. Try the homemade smoked sausage with soju mustard, kraut-chi (kimchi and kraut) and scallions tucked into a soft roll; or the kopo wangs, organic chicken wings slathered in a sweet-spicy AP sauce, laced with sesame seeds and scallions.

■ 960 W. 31st St. (bet. Farrell & Keeley Sts.)

✆ (773) 890-0588 — **WEB:** www.kimskichicago.com

■ Lunch Sun Dinner Tue – Sun   **PRICE:** 🍪

LA CASA DE SAMUEL 🍴

Mexican

🍴 | 🛋️

MAP: B3

Going strong since 1989, La Casa de Samuel continues to be a great spot for a satisfying breakfast, lunch, or dinner. The spacious, immaculate, and comfortable room features exposed brick, large windows, and oil paintings depicting the Mexican landscape. Tables and booths are filled with families enjoying platters of fragrant cooking, presented by their affable servers.

A front section of the restaurant is dedicated to making outrageously good tortillas, warm and fresh to order. The kitchen's pride and skill is clear in the chicken enchiladas, bathed in an outstanding salsa roja, served alongside refried black beans and rice studded with cubed potatoes and peas. The cabrito here is intensely tasty, perfectly seasoned, and slow-roasted with care.

■ 2834 W. Cermak Rd. (bet. California Ave. & Marshall Blvd.)
🚇 California (Pink)
✆ (773) 376-7474 — **WEB:** www.lacasadesamuel.com
■ Lunch & dinner daily   PRICE: 🍴🍴

NANA 😊

American

🍴🍴 | ♿ ☂ ⊡ 🛋️

MAP: F5

Nana Solis is the matriarch of this family-run Bridgeport favorite, whose visible kitchen and two dining rooms (one less formal) seem to be perpetually humming. A devoted breakfast crowd takes up residence at the coffee "bar" and butcher-block tables each day, often perusing the marvelous modern artwork—hung on the walls and usually for sale.

Locally sourced and organic are the guiding principles behind every ingredient here, which is given a bold Latin American bent. Avocado batons are tossed in panko, then flash-fried for a crispy exterior and creamy center. Another favorite among the "Nanadicts" is the eggs Benedict with chorizo, corn pupusas, and poblano cream. Sunday nights feature family-style fried chicken dinners fit for groups with larger appetites.

■ 3267 S. Halsted St. (at 33rd St.)
✆ (312) 929-2486 — **WEB:** www.nanaorganic.com
■ Lunch daily Dinner Wed – Sun   PRICE: $$

PLEASANT HOUSE PUB 😊

Gastropub

XX | 🍺 ♿ 🍄 🚂 🛶   **MAP:** E3

Classic English pies may be the specialty of this house, but don't let that inspire visions of chintz and tea cozies—the interiors here are decidedly modern, with marble-topped tables and hand-crafted pottery.

But the crowds come for the pies, and for good reason—they're fabulous. The crust is flaky and buttery, and the inside, hearty and satisfying. Dig into the steak and ale Royal, with its beef stew filling and side of minty peas, gravy, and mashed potatoes, and you'll be hunting for every last crumb. The comfort food hits also keep on coming, from rarebit mac and cheese with Trooper Ale cheese sauce, to fish and chips on Fridays. Of course, with much of the seasonal greens from local farms, rest assured that even a simple salad will be a revelation.

◼ 2119 S. Halstead Ave. (at 21st St.)
✆ (773) 523-7437 — **WEB:** www.pleasanthousepub.com
◼ Lunch & dinner Tue – Sun   **PRICE: $$**

THE ROSEBUD 🍴

Italian

XX | ♿ 🎪 🤝   **MAP:** D2

The Rosebud holds its own among the brass of University Village's Italian thoroughfare. The original location of what is now an extended family of restaurants throughout Chicagoland, it's nothing if not classic with its red neon sign, dark carved wood, and cool but accommodating waitstaff.

Italian wedding soup brings comfort with moist, tiny meatballs, escarole, and acini di pepe simmered in broth; while sweet sausage chunks, caramelized onions, and a garlicky white wine sauce make chicken giambotta a satisfying choice. Loyal patrons crowd around white tableclothes for platters of their favorite chicken parmesan or linguine topped with a mountain of clams. Also, dessert is not to be missed: a single slice of carrot cake will gratify the whole table.

◼ 1500 W. Taylor St. (at Laflin St.)
🚇 Polk
✆ (312) 942-1117 — **WEB:** www.rosebudrestaurants.com
◼ Lunch & dinner daily   **PRICE: $$**

RIVER NORTH

Urban, picture-perfect, and always-happening River North not only edges the Magnificent Mile, but is also set north of the Chicago River, just across the bridge from the Loop. Once packed with factories and warehouses, today this capital of commercialization is the ultimate landing place for art galleries, well-known restaurants, swanky shopping, and a hopping nightlife. Thanks to all this versatility, the area attracts literally everybody—from lunching ladies and entrepreneurs, to tour bus-style visitors.

Tourists are sure to drop by, if only to admire how even mammoth chain restaurants ooze a particular charm here. Among them is **Rock 'n' Roll McDonald's**, a block-long, music-themed outpost of the ubiquitous burger chain. This is one of the world's busiest **MickeyD's** with an expanded menu, music memorabilia, and bragging rights to the first two-lane drive-through. Speaking of drive-throughs, River North is also home to the original **Portillo's**, a hot dog, burger, and beer favorite, whose giant exterior belies its efficient service and better-than-expected food. When it

comes to the size, few buildings can rival **Merchandise Mart** (so large it once had its own ZIP code), known for its retail stores, drool-worthy kitchen showrooms, and two great food shops. **Artisan Cellar** is one such gem where in addition to boutique wines and cheeses, you can also purchase Katherine Anne Confections' fresh cream caramels. Locals also adore and routinely frequent **The Chopping Block** for its expertly taught themed cooking courses; updated, well-edited wine selections; and sparkling knife collection.

From trends to legends, **Carson's** is a barbecue institution. This squat brick box has no windows, but is just the kind of place where wise guys like to do business, with a bib on of course! This old-school treasure features framed pictures of every local celebrity, who can also be seen gracing the walls at seafood superstar, **Shaw's Crab House**. Their nostalgic bar and dining den is dotted with stainless steel bowls to collect the shells from the multitude of bottom-dwellers on offer. Crab is always available of course, but selections spin with the season. For those who aren't down with seafood in any form, this kitchen turns out a few prime steaks as well. Combat the bitter-cold winters and warm your soul with hearty food and easy elegance at **Lawry's Prime Rib** in the 1890's McCormick Mansion. Inside, the opulent dining room covers all bases from prime rib dinners to seafood signatures. But true carnivores who like their meat and potatoes done in grand style will find deep comfort in **Smith & Wollensky's** elaborate carte. Another nationwide chain, **Fleming's Prime Steakhouse & Wine Bar** is as well-regarded and recognizable as the aromas wafting from **Bow Truss Coffee Roasters**, where busy commuters pop in for a robust espresso. Further indulge your dessert dreams at **Firecakes Donuts** where coconut cream-filled buns are chased down by piping-hot chocolate bobbing with soft marshmallows. The Windy City's doughnut craze then carries on at **Doughnut Vault**, brought to you by restaurateur Brendan Sodikoff, who appears to have the Midas touch with this morning fried dough. Formerly the location for the infamous Cabrini-Green government housing, today **Chicago Lights: Urban Farm** showcases organic produce, nutritional education, and workforce training, thereby elevating the level of economic opportunities available to this vibrant community. On the other hand, **Eataly** is an impressive ode to Italian food, employing a massive workforce. This gourmet emporium may present the same delicacies as its NYC flagship, but the Nutella (counter) with its mouthwatering selection is bound to have masses returning for more.

DEEP-DISH DELIGHTS

Thanks to its wide-ranging and diverse community, River North is also a great destination for myriad food genres, including the local phenomenon of deep-dish pizza. With a doughy crust cradling abundant cheese, flavorful sauce, and a number of other toppings, some may say this is closer to a casserole or "hot dish" than an Italian-style pizza. Either way, these pies take a while to craft, so be prepared to wait wherever you go. **Pizzeria Uno** (or sister **Pizzeria Due**), and **Giordano's** are some of the best-known pie makers in town. And if a little indigestion isn't a concern, follow up these decadent delights with yet another local specialty, namely the Italian beef. At **Mr. Beef's**, these "parcels" resemble a messy, yet super-tasty French dip, wrapping thinly sliced beef with hot or sweet peppers on a hoagie. If you order it "wet," both the meat and bread will be dipped in pan juices. You could also add cheese, but hey, this isn't Philly! Distinguished by day, River North pumps up the volume at night with sleek cocktail lounges, night clubs, and Irish bars. Slip into **Three Dots and a Dash**, a retro, tiki-inspired spot featuring some of the city's most well-regarded mixologists. But for a more rootin'-tootin' good time, stop by the electric **Underground Wonder Bar**, whose dangerously tenacious punch-bowls and crowd-pleasing menu make it a favorite for private parties. Meanwhile, happy hour is always hopping at **Green Door Tavern**, which gets its name from the fact that its colored front told Prohibition-era customers where to enter for a drink. To appreciate what all the fuss is about, order the "famous corned beef sandwich" or the "legend burger" and leave with a smile.

River North

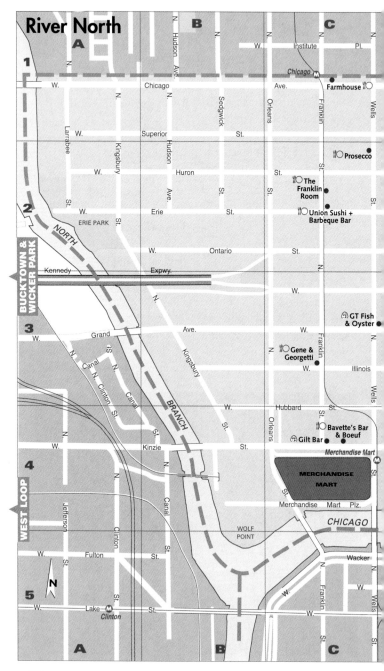

Farmhouse ○

Prosecco ○

The Franklin Room ○

Union Sushi + Barbeque Bar ○

GT Fish & Oyster ●

Gene & Georgetti ○

Bavette's Bar & Boeuf ○

Gilt Bar ●

MERCHANDISE MART

CHICAGO

WOLF POINT

BUCKTOWN & WICKER PARK

WEST LOOP

N

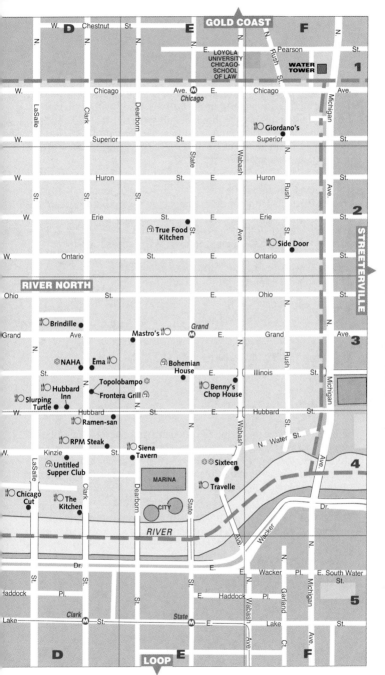

D W. Chestnut St. **E** **F**

Pearson St.

W. LOYOLA UNIVERSITY CHICAGO-SCHOOL OF LAW

WATER TOWER **1**

W. Chicago Ave. Ⓜ E. Chicago Ave.
Chicago

Giordano's

W. Superior St. E. Superior St.

W. Huron St. Huron St.

W. Erie St. E. Erie St.

True Food Kitchen

Side Door

W. Ontario St. E. Ontario St.

STREETERVILLE

Ohio St. E. Ohio St.

Brindille

Grand Ave. Mastro's *Grand* Ⓜ E. Grand Ave. **3**

NAHA Ema Bohemian House

Illinois St.

Topolobampo Benny's Chop House

Hubbard Inn Frontera Grill

Slurping Turtle

W. Hubbard St. E. Hubbard St.

Ramen-san

RPM Steak Siena Tavern

N. Water St.

Kinzie Sixteen **4**

Untitled Supper Club

MARINA Travelle

Chicago Cut The Kitchen

CITY

Dr.

RIVER

Wacker Ave.

Dr.

E. Wacker Pl. E. South Water St. **5**

Haddock Pl.

E. Haddock Pl. Garland

Clark Ⓜ St. *State* Ⓜ E. Lake St.

Lake

D **E** **F**

BAVETTE'S BAR & BOEUF 🍴

Steakhouse

✗✗ | 🍸 ♿ 🧼
MAP: C4

With a sultry jazz soundtrack and speakeasy ambience, this swanky destination is unfailingly packed every evening with a boisterous crowd. The feel inside may be dark and loud, but that only adds to the bonhomie of the chic and cavernous den, outfitted with exposed brick walls, mismatched dangling light fixtures, and tobacco-brown Chesterfield-style sofas.

Steakhouse and raw bar standards dominate the menu. Most steaks are wet-aged and though some may prefer more funk, the cuts are expertly broiled. Perfectly rendered steak frites served with a buttery béarnaise sauce is a great way to go. But, the kitchen deserves praise for other, more unexpected options like fresh-baked crab cake with remoulade; or creamy short rib stroganoff bobbing with hand-cut pasta.

▨ 218 W. Kinzie St. (bet. Franklin & Wells Sts.)
🚇 Merchandise Mart
🕽 (312) 624-8154 — **WEB:** www.bavetteschicago.com
▨ Dinner nightly
PRICE: $$$

BENNY'S CHOP HOUSE 🍴

Steakhouse

✗✗✗ | 🍸 🍺 🧼
MAP: E3

Old-school service meets modern elegance at Benny's Chop House. A far cry from the clubby, masculine steakhouses of yesteryear and just a stone's throw from the Magnificent Mile, this expansive but welcoming space goes for understated glamour, with tasteful inlaid wood and burgundy columns offset by natural stone walls, white birch branches, and a marble bar.

Though Benny's steaks are the draw, those prime cuts of filet mignon and ribeye are matched by fresh seafood like simply roasted bone-in halibut fillet and classic raw bar towers, along with a variety of pastas and salads. A trio of sliders featuring mini portions of Benny's burger, crab cake, and sliced filet with horseradish cream elevates the idea of bar snacks to new heights.

▨ 444 N. Wabash Ave. (bet. Hubbard & Illinois Sts.)
🚇 Grand (Red)
🕽 (312) 626-2444 — **WEB:** www.bennyschophouse.com
▨ Lunch & dinner daily
PRICE: $$$

BOHEMIAN HOUSE 🐸
Eastern European

XX | 🍸 🍶 🍺🥄   **MAP:** E3

This wickedly stylish "house" is exactly what River North needed to shake it up—a truly unique restaurant serving delicious Czech, Austrian, and Hungarian cuisines. The stunning beer hall-meets-art nouveau interior (think reclaimed wood beams, stunning tiles arching over a semi-open kitchen, sky-blue tufted leather couches, and Persian rugs) is worth a visit alone. No detail is overlooked.

Delightfully, the food is amazingly tasty and just as pretty to look at. Don't miss the open-faced schnitzel sandwich, highlighting juicy pork over apple and kohlrabi slaw, aged Gouda, a fried egg, and drizzle of coarse mustard. Also a must do? The warm blueberry kolacky, a traditional Czech cookie filled with blueberry coulis and served with lemon curd and blueberry-sour cream ice cream.

◻ 11 W. Illinois St. (bet. Dearborn & State Sts.)
🚇 Grand (Red)
✆ (312) 955-0439 — **WEB:** www.bohochicago.com
◻ Lunch Thu – Sun   Dinner nightly   **PRICE:** $$

BRINDILLE 🍴
French

XxX | 🖐   **MAP:** D3

This posh bistro is located just steps away from NAHA, it's impressive sister restaurant from cousins Carrie and Michael Nahabedian. Hushed and intimate, the dining room is awash with a palette of soothing greys and dressed up with herringbone floors along with black-and-white photography.

Brindille's menu isn't a sequel to NAHA's contemporary Mediterranean fare, but instead bears a strong Parisian accent influenced by the chef's love of French cuisine. Roasted chestnuts are whirled into a creamy soup and poured over compressed apple, wild mushrooms, and puffed rice. Spot-on Dover sole meunière is plated with a purée of watercress and golden-crisp pommes rissolées. And for dessert, preserved cherries are just one option to fill the baked-to-order almond clafoutis.

◻ 534 N. Clark St. (bet. Grand Ave. & Ohio St.)
🚇 Grand (Red)
✆ (312) 595-1616 — **WEB:** www.brindille-chicago.com
◻ Dinner Mon – Sat   **PRICE:** $$$$

CHICAGO CUT ¶○
Steakhouse

✗✗ | 🍴 ♿ 🏠 🖥 📠 🛋

MAP: D4

Chicago Cut is a steakhouse perfectly suited for the City of the Big Shoulders. The finely tailored locale bustles day and night, thanks to being wrapped in windows along the riverfront, sumptuous red leather furnishings, warm wood trim, and a crackerjack service team cementing its steakhouse vibe.

Non-meat entrées include cedar-planked salmon with a sriracha-honey glaze, but make no mistake: beef is boss here. Prime steaks, butchered and dry-aged in-house for 35 days, get just the right amount of time under the flame, as is the case with the perfectly cooked-to-order Porterhouse—pre-sliced and plated for each guest. Sides are a must and should include the dome of hashbrowns, creamed spinach redolent of nutmeg, or tender stalks of grilled asparagus.

▪ 300 N. LaSalle St. (at Wacker Dr.)
🚇 Merchandise Mart
☎ (312) 329-1800 — **WEB:** www.chicagocutsteakhouse.com
▪ Lunch & dinner daily   PRICE: $$$

ĒMA ¶○
Mediterranean

✗✗ | ♿ 🛋

MAP: D3

Cross the threshold into this breezy, elegant space—all whitewashed brick, wood-slat windows, and lush greenery—and prepare to be transported to the shores of the Adriatic.

The menu boasts an array of fresh, healthy Greek and Middle Eastern dishes, like smoky charred eggplant spread, tempting cold mezzes, and a variety of kebabs. And it should come as no surprise that these items taste as though they were prepared in a cozy home kitchen, as Ēma translates to "mother" in Hebrew. Dig into the lamb and beef kefta, a plate of perfectly grilled, skewered meat served alongside tasty zhoug, a spicy herb and chile pepper relish. Then cool off with a few spoonfuls of delightfully tart frozen yogurt before booking your return ticket home to the Midwest.

▪ 74 W. Illinois St. (at Clark St.)
🚇 Grand (Red)
☎ (312) 527-5586 — **WEB:** www.emachicago.com
▪ Lunch & dinner daily   PRICE: $$

FARMHOUSE ⵠ

Gastropub

❌ | 🍺 ♿ 🏞 🛋️   **MAP:** C1

Like shaking the hand of your local farmer, grab the pitchfork door handles of Farmhouse and you'll be almost as close to the source of your food. Much of the décor is salvaged and much of the menu is procured right from the Midwest. From Indiana chicken to Michigan wine, local is more than a buzzword. Exposed brick, rough-hewn wood, and wire-encased filament bulbs make it the quintessential modern tavern.

Highlights of the harvest headline each course. Whole-grain mustard dresses up a vibrant (and requisite) beet salad. Nueske's bacon is the star in a rustic BLT, accompanied by Klug Farms peaches tossed with balsamic dressing. Cream cheese-frosted carrot bread pudding is fragrant from autumn spices, layered with a golden raisin purée and nutmeg crunch.

- 228 W. Chicago Ave. (bet. Franklin & Wells Sts.)
- Chicago (Brown)
- (312) 280-4960 — **WEB:** www.farmhousechicago.com
- Lunch & dinner daily   **PRICE:** $$

THE FRANKLIN ROOM ⵠ

American

❌❌ | ♿ 🏞 🖥 🤝   **MAP:** C2

With a motto like "Ladies and Gentlemen Welcome," it's no surprise that the subterranean space housing this modern-day tavern and whiskey bar is as inviting as they come. Surrounded by backlit bottles of top-notch spirits under wrought-iron latticework light panels, guests gather for convivial conversation and great drinks.

Fans of Bourbon will delight in the Derby Day Mule, which swaps out vodka for Buffalo Trace. Pair your libation with rib-sticking dishes like a sandwich of garlic- and balsamic vinegar-roasted portobello mushroom caps layered with a runny egg, grilled tomato, and blue cheese; or a steaming bowl of braised duck soup complete with thick and silky pappardelle. End on a high note—think Bourbon-infused milkshake with house-made ice cream.

- 675 N. Franklin St. (bet. Erie & Huron Sts.)
- Chicago (Brown)
- (312) 445-4686 — **WEB:** www.franklinroom.com
- Lunch Mon – Fri Dinner nightly   **PRICE:** $$

FRONTERA GRILL 🐸

Mexican

✕✕ | 🍹 🏯 🖼 🗞 🖽   **MAP:** D3

The linchpin in Rick Bayless' empire, Frontera Grill is decidedly unique in its homage to regional Mexican cuisine and displays a near cult-like devotion to local product. The service at this dining room, psychedelic in its color scheme, can verge on vapid, but find a seat on the bar side for a warmer (and worthier) experience.

The ever-changing menu is cohesive with a mix of classics and specialties like sopa azteca, a nourishing pasilla chile broth poured atop crisp tortilla strips, cool avocado, grilled chicken, and jack cheese. A version of the classic from Morelia, enchiladas a la plaza are first flash-fried, then folded over seasoned cabbage, potatoes, and carrots. Pair this plate with a side of spinach in green chile and you won't be unhappy. Ever.

🔲 445 N. Clark St. (bet. Hubbard & Illinois Sts.)
🚇 Grand (Red)
📞 (312) 661-1434 — **WEB:** www.rickbayless.com
🔲 Lunch & dinner Tue – Sat   **PRICE: $$**

GENE & GEORGETTI 🍴

Steakhouse

✕✕ | ♿ 🖼 🖽   **MAP:** C3

No, it's not a Hollywood set. This Italian-American steak joint is the real thing, and those wiseguys at the bar have been clinking their ice cubes in this wood-paneled room for decades. The historic spot, founded in 1941, is boisterous downstairs with the aforementioned regulars and guys grabbing a bite; upstairs is more refined for local politico lunches and a bit of old-school romance at dinner.

Gene & Georgetti is a steakhouse with an Italian bloodline, prominently displayed in the heaping helping of fried peperoncini and bell peppers with the signature "chicken alla Joe." The cottage fries (oversized potato planks that come with most entrées) might necessitate a doggie bag, but all the better to leave room for a slice of classic carrot cake.

🔲 500 N. Franklin St. (at Illinois St.)
🚇 Merchandise Mart
📞 (312) 527-3718 — **WEB:** www.geneandgeorgetti.com
🔲 Lunch & dinner Mon – Sat   **PRICE: $$$$**

GILT BAR 😊

Gastropub

✗✗ | 🍸 🍺 ♿ 🏕 ⬜ 🤚   **MAP:** C4

It's not easy to miss the revolving door entrance to Gilt Bar, a moody and imposing retreat. The bar up front mixes cocktails to a metronomic rhythm, while the back feels more intimate with studded leather banquettes and nostalgic lighting.

However make no mistake: this is no Bugsy Malone speakeasy, but a grown-up version for aficionados with astute palates. Snack on smoky Brussels sprouts finished with a Dijon vinaigrette and dusting of pecorino before savoring ricotta gnocchi tossed in nutty brown butter sauce with butternut squash, chives and parmesan. For the finale, diner-style pies are all the rage. Gorge on a coconut-cream rendition topped with pleasantly bitter coffee-infused ice cream and chocolate sauce—perhaps to the tunes of Bob Dylan? Bliss.

🔲 230 W. Kinzie St. (at Franklin St.)
🏛 Merchandise Mart
📞 (312) 464-9544 — **WEB:** www.giltbarchicago.com
🔲 Dinner nightly   **PRICE:** $$

GIORDANO'S 🍴

Pizza

✗   **MAP:** F1

Value, friendly service, and delicious deep-dish pizza make Giordano's a crowd sweetheart. With locations dotting the city and suburbs, this restaurant has been gratifying locals with comforting Chicago-style Italian-American fare for years. Come during the week—service picks up especially at dinner—to avoid the cacophony.

The menu includes your typical salads and pastas, but you'd do well to save room for the real star: the deep-dish. Bring backup because this pie could feed a small country. The spinach version arrives on a buttery pastry crust, filled with sautéed (or steamed) spinach with tomato sauce, and topped with mozzarella and parmesan. For those cold, windy nights, opt for delivery—their website sketches a detailed menu.

🔲 730 N. Rush St. (at Superior St.)
🏛 Chicago (Red)
📞 (312) 951-0747 — **WEB:** www.giordanos.com
🔲 Lunch & dinner daily   **PRICE:** ⊖

GT FISH & OYSTER

Seafood

XX | MAP: C3

Quaint seaside shacks have nothing on this nautical-chic urban spot. A boomerang-shaped communal table by the raw bar makes a perfect perch for slurping oysters. Lead fishing weights keep napkins in place on brass-edged tables, arranged beneath a chalkboard mural of a jaunty swordfish skeleton. Pescatarians savor the seafood dishes meant for sharing, but those who forgo fish are limited to three meat options. Start with tuna poke dressed in soy sauce, sesame oil, and ginger with shaved cucumber. Then move on to deep-fried oysters topped with kimchi and served in a soft slider bun. Carrot cake with orange buttercream, pineapple purée, and coconut ice cream is pure bliss.

Steak lovers should stop by GT Prime, lauded for its luxurious setting and unique cuts.

531 N. Wells St. (at Grand Ave.)
Grand (Red)
(312) 929-3501 — **WEB:** www.gtoyster.com
Lunch Tue - Sun Dinner nightly **PRICE: $$**

HUBBARD INN

American

XX | MAP: D3

Handsome from head-to-toe, the Hubbard Inn takes the idea of a classic tavern and dresses it to the nines. Brass-clad globe lights glow above lacquered plank tables in the front bar room, leading to tufted leather couches and fireplaces in the book-lined and Hogwarts-worthy library. The second floor is low-slung and loungy. A wall-sized chalkboard behind the marble bar whets whistles with descriptions of cocktails.

The kitchen's shareable dishes appeal to nearly every appetite. And while ubiquitous items like lamb meatballs or grilled octopus salad lean towards the Mediterranean, Maine lobster roll or bison burger with pickled raspberries are all-American. Brunch offerings like fried chicken with buttermilk biscuits have garnered a cult-like following—natch.

110 W. Hubbard St. (bet. Clark & LaSalle Sts.)
Merchandise Mart
(312) 222-1331 — **WEB:** www.hubbardinn.com
Lunch & dinner daily **PRICE: $$**

THE KITCHEN ⅃O

American

XX | 🍸 🍺 ♿ 🖥 🛋 🖐

MAP: D4

Panoramic views and eye-popping spaces are par for the course at most of the lofty spots abutting the Chicago River, but The Kitchen's farm-to-table food manages to steer the focus back to the plate. The restaurant's approachable, community-minded take on straightforward seasonal food—along with its impressive drinks program—makes it easy to please.

Even if you're not attending a Monday "Community Night" dinner alongside many of the purveyors whose ingredients appear on the plate, you'll find a fresh, flavorful mix of dishes. Crushed white bean bruschetta is topped with a sprightly herb and frisée salad, which is in turn dressed with a blood orange vinaigrette. And wild Bristol Bay salmon is poached with care, its silkiness punctuated by garlic-chive aïoli.

■ 316 N. Clark St. (bet. Kinzie St. & the Chicago River)
🚇 Merchandise Mart
📞 (312) 836-1300 — **WEB:** www.thekitchenbistros.com
■ Lunch & dinner daily   **PRICE: $$**

MASTRO'S ⅃O

Steakhouse

XxX | 🍸 ♿ 🖥 🖐

MAP: E3

Mastro's takes its perch in the Windy City's steakhouse scene with the swagger of an old pro. Black SUVs unload VIPs in front of the revolving door, which in turn leads to a gleaming wall of bottles at the gilded bar. Live lounge music may take the level of conversation up a notch, but sip on a shaken martini to blank out the surrounding din.

Steaks on screaming hot platters come unadorned unless otherwise listed, and servers will happily rattle off recommendations for toppings, sauces, and crusts. Salads like Mastro's house version, a local favorite stocked with chopped jumbo shrimp and a giant steamed prawn, are hearty (read: oversized), but smaller portions are also on offer so you may as well leave room for their renowned butter cake.

■ 520 N. Dearborn St. (at Grand Ave.)
🚇 Grand (Red)
📞 (312) 521-5100 — **WEB:** www.mastrosrestaurants.com
■ Dinner nightly   **PRICE: $$$$**

NAHA ☘
American

XxX | ♿ ✋

After more than 15 years, NAHA is still strutting her stuff, remaining one of Chicago's most beloved dining destinations. Fans of Chef Carrie Nahabedian arrive expecting a creative, magnificent meal with exceptional service, and the kitchen consistently delivers it to a tee. There's a quiet elegance to this dining room—a sleek, window-wrapped space with contemporary accents of concrete, wood and greenery. If your idea of relaxation starts with pre-dinner drinks, the sizable bar and smattering of tables in the front lounge are an open invitation to start slow and relish the evening. It's that kind of place.

Despite its understated setting, rest assured that the seasonally driven Mediterranean cuisine is anything but. Risotto arrives studded with braised oxtail, buttery Bietina greens, preserved black truffle, scallions, and parmesan. Next, sea scallops, seemingly plucked straight from the sea, are dusted with citrus, vanilla and spices, then laid on a bed of glazed Belgian endive, and finally accompanied by spearmint, celery fronds, pea shoots, and grapefruit.

A Concord grape tart featuring pistachio-dusted meringue, tarragon, lemon rind and pistachio ice cream makes a powerful finish.

▪ 500 N. Clark St. (at Illinois St.)
🏙 Grand (Red)
☏ (312) 321-6242 — **WEB:** www.naha-chicago.com
▪ Lunch Tue – Fri   Dinner Mon – Sat   PRICE: $$$

PROSECCO 🍴○

Italian

XxX | 🏠 ⬚ 🧼

MAP: C2

No matter the hour, it's always time for bubbly at Prosecco, where a complimentary splash of the namesake Italian sparkler starts each meal. This fizzy wine inspires the restaurant's elegant décor, from creamy pale walls and damask drapes to travertine floors. Sit at the long wooden bar or in one of the well-appointed dining rooms for a second glass chosen from the long list of frizzante and spumante wines.

Hearty dishes spanning the many regions of Italy cut through the heady bubbles. Carpaccio selections include the classic air-dried bresaola as well as whisper-thin seared rare duck breast. Saltimbocca di vitello marries tender veal medallions with crispy Prosciutto di Parma and creamy mozzarella, with hints of sage in the tomato-brandy sauce.

- 710 N. Wells St. (bet. Huron & Superior Sts.)
- Chicago (Brown)
- (312) 951-9500 — **WEB:** www.prosecco.us.com
- Lunch Mon – Fri   Dinner Mon – Sat

PRICE: $$

RAMEN-SAN 🍴○

Asian

X

MAP: D4

Lettuce Entertain You brings you bowlfuls of ingredient-driven noodle soups served up right next door to the restaurant group's Il Porcellino. The menu at this Asian concept revolves around a handful of tastefully crafted broths dancing with Tokyo wavy noodles produced by Sun Noodle. The tonkotsu ramen is a traditional pleasure afloat with sweet slices of chashu, wakame, and molten egg. Meanwhile, the kimchi and fried chicken ramen is a novel departure, defined by pungent fried garlic and buttered corn.

Ramen-san's loyal following is comprised of hipsters and suits alike, and they all seem to dig the salvaged look and booming playlist. Night owls take note: Japanese whiskies rule the bar and fried rice is served late into the night.

- 59 W. Hubbard St. (bet. Clark & Dearborn Sts.)
- Grand (Red)
- (312) 377-9950 — **WEB:** www.ramensan.com
- Lunch & dinner daily

PRICE: ⊗⊗

RPM STEAK 🍴

Steakhouse

XxX | 😎 🖥 📱   **MAP:** D4

RPM Steak shares the same sleek, moneyed vibe as still-happening RPM Italian, its sister restaurant located just around the corner. Polished black, white, and wood décor speaks to the finer things in life, with a menu of succulent steaks, raw bar offerings, and sides to back it up. For the best people-watching, score one of the semicircular booths edging the room.

A massive single tiger prawn, served simply on ice with lemon, is a tasty, visually stunning starter. Steaks range from petite filets to dry-aged 24-ounce cowboy cuts with a list of big reds to match. Highlights include the classic, deeply satisfying steak frites, tender and pink inside, charred outside, and complemented by truffle béarnaise for the meat and Caesar dip for the fries.

▨ 66 W. Kinzie St. (bet. Clark & Dearborn Sts.)
🚇 Merchandise Mart
📞 (312) 284-4990 — **WEB:** www.rpmsteak.com
▨ Lunch Mon – Fri   Dinner nightly   **PRICE:** $$$$

SIDE DOOR 🍴

Gastropub

XX | 🍺   **MAP:** F2

In a city with no shortage of steakhouses, Side Door dares to be different. It's the casual arm of Lawry's in the historic McCormick Mansion, offering the same quality and service without the power lunch vibe. Comfy leather banquettes and wide wooden tables are well spaced throughout the bi-level restaurant, offering a respite for shoppers to relax with a cheese plate and craft beer flight.

Share an order of prime rib poutine among friends—it's drenched in beef gravy and pepper jack cheese—or go whole hog with the prime rib sandwich, which is hand-carved to order and presented tableside with horseradish cream and au jus. For something lighter but just as pleasurable, try the kale Caesar, with white anchovies and a delicately creamy garlic dressing.

▨ 100 E. Ontario St. (at Rush St.)
🚇 Grand (Red)
📞 (312) 787-6768 — **WEB:** www.sidedoorchicago.com
▨ Lunch & dinner daily   **PRICE:** $$

SIENA TAVERN ⅋○

Italian

✗✗ | ♿ ⌖ ⟳ ⬚ ⟋ ⬚

With a glitzy bar and cozy semicircular booths, this is where rustic Italian meets contemporary glam. The service and vibe are warmer than the pizza oven open to the room. There is something for everyone on this menu, including an expansive selection of antipasti, salads, and pasta. Seasonal soups are excellent, like the smooth roasted butternut squash drizzled with truffle-chestnut gremolata.

Pizzas arrive with a thin, fire-licked crust that is gently charred and puffed, perhaps creatively topped with a sauce-free mix of caramelized Brussels sprouts, roasted garlic, corn, gooey Taleggio, and white truffle oil.

Brunch-time monkey bread is so sticky, sweet and oozing with caramel, candied hazelnuts, and whipped cream, that it must be eaten with a spoon.

▦ 51 W. Kinzie St. (at Dearborn Pkwy.)
🏛 Merchandise Mart
✆ (312) 595-1322 — **WEB:** www.sienatavern.com
▦ Lunch & dinner daily   **PRICE:** $$

SLURPING TURTLE ⅋○

Japanese

✗ | ♿

MAP: D3

Both turtles and noodles symbolize longevity, so a meal here should add a few years to your life (and warmth to your belly). Inside, diners sit elbow-to-elbow at sleek communal tables, but there are also a handful of booths along one wall as well as a glass mezzanine with a view of the dining room below. Boutique beverages like Hitachino Nest beer and Ramuné bubble-gum soda bring smiles to patrons in the know.

The menu of Japanese comfort food is compact, featuring a few ramen bowls, sashimi, maki, as well as hot and cold small plates for snacking and sharing. Then bao filled with smoky-glazed pork belly and pickled veggies arrive fluffy and piping hot, while deep-fried Brussels sprouts are crispy outside, tender inside, and finished with fried shallots.

▦ 116 W. Hubbard St. (bet. Clark & LaSalle Sts.)
🏛 Merchandise Mart
✆ (312) 464-0466 — **WEB:** www.slurpingturtle.com
▦ Lunch & dinner daily   **PRICE:** ㊜

SIXTEEN ⍟ ⍟
Contemporary

XxxX | 🍸 ♿ 🍽 🛎 🥂

MAP: E4

Despite the arrival of a new chef, the cuisine at Sixteen retains a certain poetry and romance. In fact, dinner here is contemplative, delicious, and never formulaic. Dishes consistently weave French and Italian sensibilities, and showcase Asian ingredients to stunning effect.

There are two menu choices here, with optional wine pairings that change dramatically with each season. However numerous the courses, guests still leave with a sense of balance and harmony. While breakfast and lunch are also on offer, it is at dinnertime that this kitchen's talent truly shines. Specifically, its use of herbs and aromatics lightens every taste, so an opening trio of crab is sure to make the most of corn with nasturtium petals and leaves. Then spring may yield delicate Chinook salmon with roasted fiddleheads and sorrel purée, while summer presents a gently cured then briefly torched hiramasa, colorfully arranged with jade-green fennel juice.

Located on the 16th floor of the Trump International Hotel, this space impresses by virtue of a glass-enclosed foyer lined with wine bottles, African rosewood, and a Swarovski chandelier that hangs over the dining room like an inverted wedding cake.

■ 401 N. Wabash Ave. (bet. Hubbard St. & the Chicago River)
🚇 State/Lake
✆ (312) 588-8030 — **WEB:** www.trumpchicagohotel.com
■ Lunch daily Dinner Wed – Sun   PRICE: $$$$

TRAVELLE 🍴

Mediterranean

XxX | 🦀 ♿ 🖥 🛋 🛌 🤚   **MAP:** E4

This contemporary Mediterranean dining room shares its home—a landmark Mies van der Rohe tower completed in 1972—with The Langham hotel. Floor-to-ceiling windows on the second-floor space offer views of Marina City, but with its stunning kitchen displayed behind gradient glass panels, the scene inside is equally dramatic.

Creative add-ins bring flair and flavor to flawlessly executed and gorgeously composed dishes. A perfect, toothsome champagne risotto is enlivened by juicy, barely pickled grapes and toasted Marcona almonds, while a thick, creamy tranche of seared salmon rests on "healthy" fried green farro, finished with a tangy drizzle of spicy soy-mustard. Raspberry coulis and meringue shards are an ideal garnish for a fresh and zesty citrus tart.

- 🔲 330 N. Wabash Ave. (bet. Kinzie St. & the Chicago River)
- 🚇 Grand (Red)
- ✆ (312) 923-7705 — **WEB:** www.travellechicago.com
- 🔲 Lunch & dinner daily   **PRICE:** $$$

TRUE FOOD KITCHEN 😊

American

XX | ♿ 🛋   **MAP:** E2

True Food Kitchen is just what the doctor ordered—Dr. Andrew Weil, that is, who, along with «restopreneur» Sam Fox, has written a prescription for food that is as healthy as it is delicious.

Housed in a trendy part of the city and in an 8,000-square-foot loft-like space, this open and airy «kitchen» features lime-green banquettes, lemon-hued chairs, and a bar that slings fresh juice cocktails like skinny citrus margaritas. The menu showcases the chef's talent for delivering next-level vegetable dishes. But carnivores may rest easy as the gluten-free chicken sausage pie, as well as the spaghetti squash casserole topped with fresh mozzarella and dressed with herbs, caramelized onions, and shredded zuchinni, are bound to sate every type of palate.

- 🔲 1 W. Erie St. (at State St.)
- 🚇 Grand (Red)
- ✆ (312) 204-6981 — **WEB:** www.truefoodkitchen.com
- 🔲 Lunch & dinner daily   **PRICE:** $$

TOPOLOBAMPO ❀

Mexican

XX | 🍸 🍽 🤳

MAP: D3

Given its recent renovation, the scale of this jewel in the Bayless crown remains largely the same, and welcomes a rush of serious diners for original south-of-the-border food with an upscale twist. While you still have to walk through cacophonous Frontera Grill to arrive here, the relative serenity that greets you is worth the detour. This bright and cheery dining room feels worlds away from the fiesta upfront, featuring windows draped with gold curtains and colorful artwork.

The regional Mexican cuisine boasts a panoply of flavors, colors, and textures that are refined yet respect authenticity. Lunches are laid-back and include a quartet of quesadillas stuffed with chorizo, black beans and queso fresco. These are made even more luscious when served with a Veracruz salsa negra. Dinners demonstrate the full range of the kitchen's capabilities, and unveil hiramasa slices temptingly arranged with petals of ripe mango and deliciously balanced by a brick-red jackfruit and chipotle sauce.

There is no secret that cocktails here are noteworthy (margarita, anyone?), but teetotalers get equal attention thanks to sweet and tangy agua frescas splashed with tropical juices that are among the best in town.

▨ 445 N. Clark St. (bet. Hubbard & Illinois Sts.)

🚉 Grand (Red)

✆ (312) 661-1434 — **WEB:** www.rickbayless.com

▨ Lunch Tue – Fri   Dinner Tue – Sat

PRICE: $$$$

UNION SUSHI + BARBEQUE BAR 🍴

Japanese

XX | 🍸 🍺 🍶 ♿ 🏛   **MAP:** C2

The slogan of this big, bustling restaurant is "Uniting Japanese culinary tradition with a distinctly American persona," which roughly translates to "Japanese food with a party hat on." The cocktails are good, the noise levels are high, and there are more tattoos in this room than at a Yakuza convention.

The menu will take forever to read so just go directly to their two specialties—the assorted sushi rolls, some of which use black rice, and meats and fish expertly cooked over an open flame on the seriously hot robata. The ingredients are good and the flavor combinations don't get silly. Just remember that sharing is the key to keeping that final check in check, especially as the T-shirted staff with iPads, are masters of upselling.

🟦 230 W. Erie St. (at Franklin St.)
🚇 Chicago (Brown)
📞 (312) 662-4888 — **WEB:** www.eatatunion.com
🟦 Lunch Mon – Fri   Dinner nightly   **PRICE:** $$

UNTITLED SUPPER CLUB 😊

Contemporary

XX | 🍸 ♿ 🎐 🏛 🍽   **MAP:** D4

An unmarked entrance leads the way to this sultry subterranean lair, its various rooms pumping out music and serving up handcrafted cocktails to a young, sexy clientele lounging in tufted leather banquettes. Lights are nice and sultry, tables are low-slung and casual, and there are no less than 507 whiskeys to choose from.

A charcuterie board may offer up silky duck rillettes, shot through with foie gras; textured and spreadable liverwurst; as well as thin slices of prosciutto and coppa accompanied by a house-made mostarda. Overstuffed squash blossom rellenos are filled with creamy ricotta and served over agave-spiked corn relish and chili-lime crema. Don't miss the scrumptious meatloaf sandwich, slathered with Korean-style ketchup, and laced with rosemary-infused aïoli.

🟦 111 W. Kinzie St. (bet. Clark & LaSalle Sts.)
🚇 Merchandise Mart
📞 (312) 880-1511 — **WEB:** www.untitledchicago.com
🟦 Dinner Mon – Sat   **PRICE:** $$

WEST LOOP

GREEKTOWN · MARKET DISTRICT

Once home to scores of warehouses and smoke-spewing factories, the West Loop today is arguably the most booming part of the Windy City, whirring with sleek art galleries, attractive lofts, hopping nightclubs, and cool, cutting-edge restaurants. Young residents may have replaced the struggling immigrants of yore; nevertheless, traces of ethnic flavor can still be found along these vibrant blocks. They certainly aren't as dominant as before—what a difference a century or two can make—

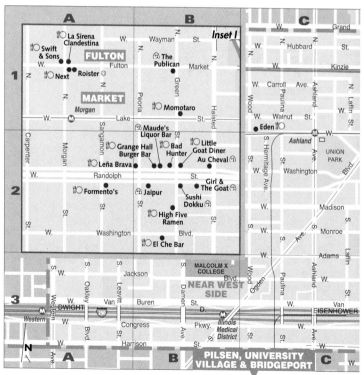

but nearby Taylor Street continues to charm passersby, tourists, and residents alike with that timeless-turned-slightly kitschy feel. Imagine the likes of delis, groceries, and food stops galore and you will start to get the picture.

A MEDITERRANEAN MARVEL

For tasty, Mediterranean-inspired munching, make your way to Greektown where everybody's Greek, even if it's just for the day. Shout "opa" at the **Taste of Greece** festival held each August, or while away an afternoon at the always-packed **Parthenon**. Its moniker may not signal ingenuity, but the menu is groaning with gyros, signature lamb dishes, and even flaming *saganaki*, thereby displaying serious showmanship. Sound all too Greek to you? Venture beyond the Mediterranean

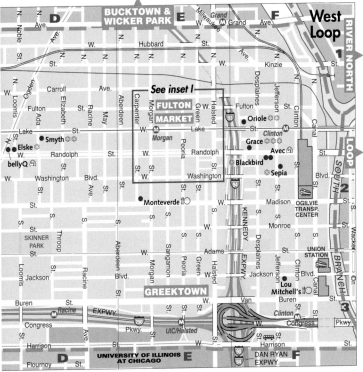

exquisite eats with intricately crafted sips at **The Aviary**. This bar in West Fulton Market is the brainchild of Chef Grant Achatz, and baby boy is quite the charmer indeed! Noted as much for its expert bartenders as well as their spherical concoctions as for its tedious reservation process (this is a Kokonas business, after all!), The Aviary is also highly devoted to product quality. For even more of a scene, head downstairs to **The Office**, a super secret and super exclusive bar, before settling in for an intimate dinner at **Next's** private dining space, **The Room**.

and into "Restaurant Row" along Randolph Street, where culinary treasures hide among beautiful, fine dining establishments. Whet your appetite with everything from sushi to subs—this mile-long sandwich breed is a best seller bursting with salty meats at **J.P. Graziano's**. Don't let their long lines deter you; you may also take your smoky temptation to **West Loop Salumi** and let their platters of glistening cured treats do the trick.

If all else fails, round-up say 1,000 of your closest friends for a meze at one of the many Moroccan spots nearby. Then chase down West Randolph's

Some carousers may choose to continue the party at **CH Distillery**, which is known to cull the finest spirits in-house. And if that's not enough, this kitchen is even known to craft such delicious small plates as potato pancakes or red caviar set atop pumpernickel blinis. Nerd alert: the name CH is a double entendre indicating the molecular formula for ethanol and Chicago's abbreviation. Rather whip it up than wolf it down? Beef up your kitchen skills at the

Calphalon Culinary Center, where groups can arrange for private hands-on instruction. After mastering the ever classic bœuf Bourguignon, get in line at **Olympia Meats**, or stroll into **Peoria Packing**, a veritable meat cooler where butchers continue to slice and dice the best cuts to order. Aspiring cooks also make the rounds to Paul Kahan's **Publican Quality Meats**, another carnivorous mecca, filled with a mind-boggling array of specialty eats that is matched only by the spectacular setting. Think: intimate cocktail gathering-meets-extravagant dinner party. For artisan food paradise savvy gourmands gather at **Dose Market**, a seasonal flea market held every Sunday, featuring the finest in food and chefs, as well as their own secret ingredients. Meanwhile, treasure hunters troll the stalls at **Chicago French Market**, an epicurean hub and multi-use arena catering to a variety of palates. Meanwhile, health nuts can't get enough of **Raw**, a grab-n-go vegan gem committed to providing the healthiest food money can buy. Moving beyond the market, even the most die-hard dieters need a lil' sugar and nearby **Glazed and Infused**, an early member of the current doughnut craze,

is sublime. Then, spice things up at the flagrantly sexy **RM Champagne Salon**.

BEER & THE BALLGAME

Hoops fans whoop it up at Bulls games at the United Center, also home to the Blackhawks. Depending on the score, the most exciting part of the night is post-game, binging with buddies over beer and bar food. **The Aberdeen Tap**, for instance, is a neighborhood hangout where everybody knows your name as well as the exceptional selection of beers on tap—they boast over 65 brews. But, be sure to also take your (more finicky) pals to **Rhine Hall**, a boutique brandy distillery run by a father-and-daughter duo. Finally, those who prefer a little brawl with their beer will fall for **Twisted Spoke**, a proverbial biker bar with tattoos and 'tudes to match. The music is loud and drinks are plentiful, but it's all in good testosterone- and alcohol-fueled fun.

AU CHEVAL 😊
American

✗ | 🍹 🍺 ♿ 🛎 🖥   **MAP:** B2

This corner bar on Randolph Street's restaurant row may be dim, but it's got a few glittering edges. The reel-to-reel in the doorway lends a retro feel, but the rest is decidedly cushy. Late-night revelers prefer to sit at tufted leather booths or savor beers at the zinc-topped bar rather than endure a wait for a table in the raucous space. Bartenders work just as hard as line cooks until the wee hours.

The kitchen puts a highfalutin spin on simple bar eats. In-house butchers craft 32-ounce pork Porterhouses for sharing; foie gras for folding into fluffy scrambled eggs; and house-made sausages for bologna sandwiches that go well beyond a kid's wildest dreams. Thin griddled cheeseburger patties are perked up by maple syrup-glazed peppered bacon.

■ 800 W. Randolph St. (at Halsted St.)
🚇 Morgan
📞 (312) 929-4580 — **WEB:** www.auchevalchicago.com
■ Lunch & dinner daily   **PRICE:** $$

AVEC 😊
Mediterranean

✗ | 🍴 🛎 🖥   **MAP:** F2

Fans have been clamoring for the dinner plates at this West Randolph mainstay for more than a decade—and now that lunch is on the menu, it's official: Avec is a non-stop hangout. It's a fun vibe, as diners are tightly packed at a long counter and communal seats in the chic wood plank-encased room; servers do a good job attending to the crowd.

Mediterranean flavors factor prominently in the kitchen's stimulating creations, like a kale and carrot salad dressed with delightfully herbaceous and spicy green harissa as well as sunflower seeds for crunch. A thick slice of excellent whole grain bread spread with walnut-beet muhamarra is the foundation of an open-faced roasted salmon sandwich. Other delights—there are many—come and go with the seasons.

■ 615 W. Randolph St. (bet. Desplaines & Jefferson Sts.)
🚇 Clinton (Green/Pink)
📞 (312) 377-2002 — **WEB:** www.avecrestaurant.com
■ Lunch Sun – Fri Dinner nightly   **PRICE:** $$

BAD HUNTER ⅋○

Contemporary

✗✗ | 🥨 🍸 🖼

MAP: B2

Bad Hunter is a wildly popular and exciting destination on this little restaurant row. The sun-filled interior is light and sleek, with a soothing décor of whitewashed brick walls, caramel-hued banquettes, and lush greenery to ensure that the space feels airy and never overcrowded. Servers deftly manage the room, no matter how many orders are rushing in.

The cooking unveils an inventive take on seasonal farm-to-table dining, with wood-fire roasting and fermentation playing large parts. Start with fluke crudo in tangy carrot-citronette, then move on to saffron farfalle dressed with an ingenious root vegetable "Bolognese" so good that no one misses the meat. Desserts are another highlight, especially the caramelized white chocolate and parsnip panna cotta.

▨ 802 W. Randolph St. (at Halsted St.)
▨ Morgan
☏ (312) 265-1745 — **WEB:** www.badhunter.com
▨ Lunch & dinner daily   **PRICE: $$**

BELLYQ 😃

Asian

✗✗ | ♿ 🀫 🧼

MAP: D2

This end of West Randolph Street might be quiet, but it's always a party inside bellyQ. The volume and energy are high throughout the lofty, concrete-heavy space with tabletop hibachi booths and industrial metal seating. A wall-length horse-themed screen separates the restaurant from casual sister spot Urban Belly, which shares the open kitchen.

As imagined by prolific Chef/owner Bill Kim, the Asian barbecue experience at bellyQ takes its form in a number of genre-melding shareable plates. A side of bibimbap-style sticky rice is crunchy and tender, tossed with glistening slices of Chinese sausage and generously sprinkled with togarashi. Chewy chunks of brownie in vanilla soft-serve are drizzled with caramel-balsamic-soy "Seoul sauce" for a savory twist.

▨ 1400 W. Randolph St. (at Ogden Ave.)
▨ Ashland (Green/Pink)
☏ (312) 563-1010 — **WEB:** www.bellyqchicago.com
▨ Dinner nightly   **PRICE: $$**

BLACKBIRD ❀

Contemporary

XX | ♿ 💧 🍴

In many ways, an acclaimed restaurant that opened in 1997 may seem like old news, but Chef/owner Paul Kahan continues to enliven this Chicago original with fresh talent and new flavor.

The space is small but packed, right down to the last lunchtime bar stool. Everything feels glossy and white, accented with high-back leather banquettes and orange place mats that pop with color at the bar. Service is sharp, busy, and handling it all very well. Meals may begin with a symphony of flavors in what appears to be a breakfast sausage patty. However, this golden-brown rabbit sausage is coarsely ground and intensely savory, fragrant with sage and pepper, set over gnocchi dressed in creamed parsley root topped with a bit of "bread and butter" pickled fennel. Slightly crisped grilled monkfish has an almost Californian sensibility, with puntarelle, shaved persimmon, sunchoke, and a dollop of green basil foam. Inspired by the yeasty baked doughnuts of the Czech Republic, Blackbird's version of kolache is light, sweet, and filled with what tastes like a perfect slice of cheesecake.

Dinner may be served as a ten-course tasting menu that shows just what this capable kitchen can do. Lunch is an astounding bargain.

▪ 619 W. Randolph St. (bet. Desplaines & Jefferson Sts.)
🚇 Clinton (Green/Pink)
✆ (312) 715-0708 — **WEB:** www.blackbirdrestaurant.com
▪ Lunch Mon – Fri   Dinner nightly   PRICE: $$$

EDEN 🍴

Contemporary

XX | ♿ 🏮 🍽️

MAP: C1

This lovely addition to the West Loop dining scene arrives thanks to husband-and-wife-team, Chef Devon Quinn and Jodi Fyfe. The gorgeous, whitewashed space offers an airy, bright ambience even by night, with exposed brick, encaustic tile at the convivial bar, tufted leather banquettes, and commissioned artwork throughout.

The inspired cuisine applies flavors of the Mediterranean to seasonal produce, some of it plucked straight from the on-site urban garden. Renowned favorites from the menu may include baked shrimp paccheri; curried lentil brik; or even cumin-grilled lamb with Israeli couscous and merguez. House-made pastas might feature sweet pea pierogi with broccoli purée, trumpet mushrooms, pickled spring onions and crispy potato shards.

◼ 1748 W. Lake St. (at Wood St.)
◼ Ashland (Green/Pink)
✆ (312) 366-2294 — **WEB:** www.edeninchicago.com
◼ Lunch Sat – Sun   Dinner Wed – Sat   **PRICE:** $$$

EL CHE BAR 🍴

Latin American

XX | ♿ 🧼

MAP: B2

This love letter to Argentine cooking arrives courtesy of Chef John Manion (of La Sirena Clandestina), who spent much of his childhood in Sao Paulo, Brazil and traveling through South America. Look beyond the obvious Checker Taxi signage to find El Che Bar hidden in plain sight. Its long, narrow space is lined with black brick, white mortar, wood slats, and leads to an enormous blazing open-hearth oven in the rear. Tiny votives and hanging tropical plants warm the room.

Big knives are a must for any good Argentinian meal, and El Che Bar is no exception. Meat plays a big role on this menu, so try the tender, braised lamb ribs, their edges charred to a beautiful crisp in the hearth, then paired with fennel salad and yogurt-mint relish.

◼ 845 W. Washington Blvd. (bet. Green & Peoria Sts.)
◼ Morgan
✆ (312) 265-1130 — **WEB:** www.elchebarchicago.com
◼ Dinner nightly   **PRICE:** $$$

ELSKE ✿

Contemporary

✕✕ | ♿ ⛱ 🖥 🧼

MAP: D2

A vivid blue neon sign marks the entry to stylish Elske, a hip and sophisticated offering brought to you by husband-and-wife chef duo, David and Anna Posey. He worked at Blackbird; she at The Publican—and what they do together in this restaurant (the name means "love" in Danish) is pure culinary magic.

The spacious setting is equal parts minimal-cool and perfectly cozy, with slate-gray concrete floors, exposed brick walls, and open ductwork. A lovely outdoor area offers an open-air campfire with two long benches and complimentary lap furs, designed for a pre- or post-dinner cocktail or two. Inside, communal tables abound and counter seats line a gleaming open kitchen, where the cooks serve dishes directly to customers.

The kitchen's deeply creative menu offers seasonal, responsibly farmed dishes rendered with impeccable skill—the flavors carefully woven together to produce irresistible profiles. A night in the talented chef duo's hands might unveil tender duck liver tart in an ethereally light buckwheat crust, paired with garlicky, salted ramps; or creamy ocean trout set over a vibrant vinaigrette with white asparagus, perfectly balanced crème fraîche, and delicate claytonia leaves.

▦ 1350 W. Randolph Ave. (at Ada St.)
🚇 Ashland (Green/Pink)
📞 (312) 733-1314 — **WEB:** www.elskerestaurant.com
▦ Dinner Wed – Sun

PRICE: $$$$

FORMENTO'S 🍴

Italian

XxX | 🕸 ♿ 🗖 🧼

MAP: A2

This fresh venue is an old soul at heart, a retro-cool den where you half expect to see Frank, Dean, and Sammy downing martinis in a corner booth. Appointed with tanned leather banquettes, crisply dressed tables, and terra-cotta-tiled floors, the scene is an enticing one in which to sup on remarkable red-sauced food.

Proving that throwback doesn't equate tired, the menu is an inspired collection of renovated favorites. Crab-and-artichoke dip arrives with house-made "Ritz" crackers; while eggplant parmesan is a fine-tuned layering of fried eggplant slices and house-pulled mozzarella that's accompanied by spaghetti draped with delicious pomodoro sauce. A refreshing spin on saltimbocca reveals pancetta-wrapped quail and leaves nothing to be desired.

▢ 925 W. Randolph St. (at Sangamon St.)
▢ Morgan
🖉 (312) 690-7295 — **WEB:** www.formentos.com
▢ Dinner nightly

PRICE: $$$

GIRL & THE GOAT 😃

Contemporary

XX | 🗖 🧼

MAP: B2

The revolving door never stops turning as Girl & The Goat's party keeps going. Even on a Monday night, guests linger for hours, shouting over the din at this sceney but always friendly stunner. Appropriately rustic wooden pillars and beams connect a warren of seating areas, from elevated platforms to banquettes to dim private corner nooks.

A pick-your-own-protein adventure, the menu is organized by ingredient with a dedicated section for goat. Start with freshly baked ham bread with smoked Swiss-cheese butter seasoned with coarse mustard and olive tapenade, then end with an almost pudding-like "all leches" cake with a scoop of strawberry-rhubarb sorbet. The kitchen will even send out mini portions of menu items for solo diners—a truly thoughtful touch.

▢ 809 W. Randolph St. (bet. Green & Halsted Sts.)
▢ Morgan
🖉 (312) 492-6262 — **WEB:** www.girlandthegoat.com
▢ Dinner nightly

PRICE: $$

GRACE ✿ ✿ ✿
Contemporary

XxxX | 🍴 ♿ 🖥 🖐

Ask passing foodies to name one of Chicago's most elegant and sophisticated restaurants and they'll probably say Grace. This room is as handsome as it is urbane and provides a supremely comfortable environment for those spending an evening discovering the culinary wizardry of Curtis Duffy.

You'll be presented with a choice between two seasonally changing menus: the vegetarian "Flora" is very good, but the omnivore "Fauna" is more impressive in every way. Opt for the wine pairings and you're finished with decision making for the night. At the center of each precisely prepared dish is the kitchen's talent for combining wonderful flavors. Trying to keep track of each delicate ingredient will nullify the benefit of the wine, so instead just marvel at the clever presentation and dig in. The cuisine is intricate and elaborately constructed, with herbs playing an integral part rather than merely acting as garnish. Occasionally your taste buds will get a little zing or slap, perhaps with the odd Thai or Vietnamese flavor, as the courses fly by.

This style of cooking is uniquely labor-intensive, so if you want to learn more, be sure to take advantage of their offer of a postprandial kitchen tour.

▨ 652 W. Randolph St. (bet. Desplaines & Halsted Sts.)
🚇 Clinton (Green/Pink)
☎ (312) 234-9494 — **WEB:** www.grace-restaurant.com
▨ Dinner Tue – Sat   **PRICE: $$$$**

GRANGE HALL BURGER BAR ⁋○

American

X | ᕹ 👫 �Ⅲ 🗐   **MAP:** B2

American Gothic accents (think Grant Wood) invade the big city at Grange Hall. A down-on-the-farm vibe is telegraphed loud and clear through swinging barn doors, quilted panels hanging above the lunch counter, and mismatched knit napkins set atop tables with wooden chairs and stools. The glassed-in pie kitchen in the back hints that dessert won't be an afterthought.

Choose your own adventure when building a burger, starting with a six- or nine-ounce grass-fed beef patty and adding toppings like Midwestern cheeses, smoked bacon, jalapeños, or homemade pickles. If a wedge of strawberry rhubarb pie or Bourbon-spiked milkshake is calling your name (especially when freshly churned ice cream is involved), go easy on those hand-cut farmhouse chili fries.

■ 844 W. Randolph St. (bet. Green & Peoria Sts.)
🚇 Morgan
✆ (312) 491-0844 — **WEB:** www.grangehallburgerbar.com
■ Lunch Tue – Sun   Dinner Tue – Sat   **PRICE:** ⌒

HIGH FIVE RAMEN ⁋○

Japanese

X   **MAP:** B2

This re-purposed industrial setting is a hipster dining hall serving two hot foodie trends under one roof. The bulk of the sprawling space is devoted to Green Street Smoked Meats, a barbecue joint where crowds of cool kids sit side-by-side downing beers and heaps of pulled pork, brisket, and Frito pie.

More worthy of attention, however, is High Five Ramen, a downstairs nook where the queue for one of its 16 seats starts early. Once inside, slurp a bowl of the signature, crazy-spicy broth. Loaded with thin alkaline noodles, a slow-cooked egg, roasted pork belly, locally grown sprouts, and black garlic oil, this unique rendition is worth the burn. For sweet, icy relief, sip on a slushy tiki cocktail—then wipe your brow and dig back in.

■ 112 N. Green St. (bet. Randolph St. & Washington Blvd.)
🚇 Morgan
✆ (312) 754-0431 — **WEB:** www.highfiveramen.com
■ Dinner nightly   **PRICE:** ⌒

JAIPUR

Indian

XX | MAP: B2

Business execs expecting the ubiquitous lunch buffet will be sorely disappointed by Jaipur—that is until they realize this popular weekday spot serves an affordable full-service lunch special that brings the buffet to your table in a parade of hammered copper katoris. In the evening, locals fill every sleek, nail-studded chair in the refined dining room as they await plates of boldly flavored Indian cooking.

The broad menu features a lengthy selection of fresh and authentically treated favorites, most of which are available as part of the bountiful lunch special. Staples on the vast à la carte menu may include aloo papdi chaat; a rich and creamy chicken korma; spiced carrot soup; and scarlet-red tandoori chicken, served with garlic naan.

847 W. Randolph St. (bet. Green & Peoria Sts.)
Morgan
(312) 526-3655 — **WEB:** www.jaipurchicago.com
Lunch & dinner daily **PRICE: $$**

LA SIRENA CLANDESTINA

Latin American

XX | MAP: A1

Chef John Manion may be splitting his time between El Che Bar and his first baby, La Sirena Clandestina, but he hasn't missed a beat. The decor reflects the location's warehouse roots through drafting stools at the bar, well-tread wood plank floors, and rugged wood tables edged in steel. Silvery pressed tin ceilings echo the happy din of conversation below.

Be sure to try the wonderful Brazilian bowl, filled with bomba rice, chimichurri, and malagueta salsa, topped with juicy grilled hangar steak (as well as avocado, grilled chicken or shrimp). Even kale salad deserves top billing, dressed with a creamy roasted poblano vinaigrette. Desserts feature a buttermilk tres leches, tender lemon-poppy seed cakes set over plum marinade and sliced market peaches.

954 W. Fulton Market (at Morgan St.)
Morgan
(312) 226-5300 — **WEB:** www.lasirenachicago.com
Lunch Fri - Sun Dinner nightly **PRICE: $$**

LEÑA BRAVA ¶◯

Mexican

XX | 🍸 🍺 ♿ ▢ 🔥   **MAP:** B2

This prime Randolph Street corner is home to a one-two punch of Rick Bayless-ness—an excellent taqueria and brewery named Cruz Blanza as well as this sophisticated cantina. An open kitchen displaying open-fire cooking is Leña Brava's stimulating focal point, while a buzzing bar pouring an encyclopedic range of agave spirits, brews from next door, and rare Mexican wines enhances the two-floor scene.

The kitchen's Northern Mexican-influenced menu combines the bounty of the sea with the primal joy of wood-fired cooking. Be tempted by icy seafood preparations like an aquachile of sashimi-grade diver scallops in spiced cucumber juice. Then consider hearth-roasted black cod al pastor with sweet and sour pineapple, coupled with heirloom corn tortillas.

▨ 900 W. Randolph St. (at Peoria St.)
🚇 Morgan
✆ (312) 733-1975 — **WEB:** www.rickbayless.com
▨ Dinner Tue – Sun   **PRICE:** $$$

LITTLE GOAT DINER ¶◯

American

XX | 🍺 ♿ ▢ 🍴 🔥   **MAP:** B2

Every neighborhood needs a good diner and in the booming West Loop, this enthusiastic homage to the reliable road trip stopover fits in perfectly. The décor gives a wink and a nod to classic design with retro booths, spinning chrome barstools, and blue-rimmed plates, but the top-quality materials keep it on the modern side. An all-day menu of amped-up faves can be had no matter the hour. Craving a shrimp cocktail at 7:00 A.M.? Five jumbo fried shrimp wrapped in somen noodles are ready to go. The Goat Almighty burger lives up to its name with fatty beef brisket, saucy pulled pork, and a ground goat patty.

Ease the pain of waiting for a table here by cooling your heels at the adjacent LG Bakery with a cup of Stumptown, a s'mores cookie, or Bloody Mary at the bar.

▨ 820 W. Randolph St. (at Green St.)
🚇 Morgan
✆ (312) 888-3455 — **WEB:** www.littlegoatchicago.com
▨ Lunch & dinner daily   **PRICE:** $$

LOU MITCHELL'S ₁O

American

✗ | 🖴   **MAP:** F3

At the top of Chicago's list of beloved names is Lou Mitchell. This eponymous diner is by no means an elegant affair, but thanks to its delicious omelets and iconic crowd, it has been on the Windy City's must-eat list since 1923. Don't panic at the length of the lines: they are long but move fast, and free doughnut holes (one of the restaurant's signature baked goods) make the wait go faster.

Back to those omelets: they may be made with mere eggs, like everyone else's, but somehow these are lighter and fluffier, almost like a soufflé, stuffed with feta, spinach, onions, or any other ingredients of your choice. They arrive in skillets with an Idaho-sized helping of potatoes. The best part? Everyone gets a swirl of soft-serve at the meal's end.

🔲 565 W. Jackson Blvd. (bet. Clinton & Jefferson Sts.)
🔲 Clinton (Blue)
🕿 (312) 939-3111 — **WEB:** www.loumitchellsrestaurant.com
🔲 Lunch daily   **PRICE:** ⬡

MAUDE'S LIQUOR BAR ☺

French

✗✗ | 🍸 ⚐ ⛱ ⟳ 🖐   **MAP:** B2

It's impossible not to love this place. The overstuffed curio cabinet and blue French metal chairs aren't true antiques, for this gorgeously disheveled and rather classy French brasserie isn't as old as the mirror's arful patina would have you believe. A handsome bar mixing contemporary and classic cocktails adds to the vintage atmosphere.

Fill up on French comfort food under the glow of mismatched crystal chandeliers, or head to the second-floor bar to snack on oysters and frites. The Lyonnaise salad is downright beautiful, tossing escarole, frisée, and baby romaine in chive vinaigrette beneath a soft boiled egg and chunks of grilled pork belly. Steak tartare satisfies from beginning to end, and the crème brûlée is a deliciously textbook finish.

🔲 840 W. Randolph St. (bet. Green & Peoria Sts.)
🔲 Morgan
🕿 (312) 243-9712 — **WEB:** www.maudesliquorbar.com
🔲 Dinner nightly   **PRICE:** $$

MOMOTARO 🍴

Japanese

✕✕ | 🍸 🍱 🤚   **MAP:** B1

Boka Restaurant Group's stunning West Loop canteen embraces a fantastical view of Japanese dining. An impressive selection of imported whiskies is listed on a retro-style departure board; a private dining room upstairs is styled to resemble a mid-century corporate boardroom; and a traditional izakaya beckons diners downstairs. Consistently packed, the impeccably designed space boasts numerous kitchens churning out a wide range of dishes.

Creative bites abound in the chef's omakase featuring torched baby squid wrapped in nori. Then a Hawaiian seaweed salad with diced nopales may be followed by robata-grilled Wagyu skirt steak with foie gras, shisito pepper, and yuzu kosho. The steamed yuzu pudding cake is just one example of the surprisingly strong dessert roster.

▦ 820 W. Lake St. (at Green St.)
🚇 Morgan
✆ (312) 733-4818 — **WEB:** www.momotarochicago.com
▦ Dinner nightly   **PRICE: $$**

MONTEVERDE 🍴

Italian

✕✕ | 🍸 ♿ ⛱   **MAP:** E2

Chef Sarah Grueneberg is a local celebrity, so expect her offspring to be packed to the last dining counter stool by 5:30 P.M. Then again this is prime seating, because behind that wood-grain bar lies the pasta station where sheets are rolled, cut, and hung to dry before appearing on your plate. Her signature Italian cooking—or cucina tipica as the menu lists it—is what draws crowds.

That said, this menu is about more than pasta, beginning with an extraordinary yet humble vessel displaying neat little bundles of cabbage leaves stuffed with herbed breadcrumbs and mushrooms, served in an inky-dark porcini Bolognese. "Wok-fried" orecchiette are pleasantly toothsome, slicked with spicy tomato sauce, and topped with gorgeously fresh head-on shrimp.

▦ 1020 W. Madison St. (at Carpenter St.)
🚇 Morgan
✆ (312) 888-3041 — **WEB:** www.monteverdechicago.com
▦ Dinner Tue – Sun   **PRICE: $$**

NEXT 🍴
Contemporary

✗✗ | 📷 🖐️   **MAP:** A1

Welcome to dinner as theater, where the only thing more radical than each new theme is the success (or failure) of the cuisine. Whether you come for meals that recreate ancient Rome, Hollywood, or The World's 50 Best, it makes a fun night.

Last year, The French Laundry enthusiasts came to relive the moment when a young upstart chef named Grant Achatz started cooking there 20 years ago. Do guests mistake Next's rendition for Chef Keller's signature "oysters and pearls"? Probably not. But clearly, this is a different kitchen with its own unique skill and talent—the proof is in the downright perfect rabbit saddle. Guests even left with that trademark wooden clothespin that listed Next alongside The French Laundry logo—their dedication to detail is unwavering.

◼ 953 W. Fulton Market (at Morgan St.)
🚇 Morgan
🖉 N/A — **WEB:** www.nextrestaurant.com
◼ Dinner Wed – Sun   **PRICE:** $$$$

THE PUBLICAN 👻
Gastropub

✗✗ | 🍺 ♿ 🛖 🖐️   **MAP:** B1

This Fulton Market stalwart is something of a local legend and the flagship of Paul Kahan's restaurant empire. Inspired by century-old public houses where political conversations and beer flowed with equal fervor, The Publican remains true to its roots with cloistered wood booths, a brass bar, and background music that cannot be heard over the patrons' happy din.

As expected from the portraits of pigs displayed throughout the room, pork takes precedence here with spicy rinds, potted rillettes, or grilled Berkshire pork collar with watermelon, tomatoes, burnt chili, and dill. No matter what you order, pair it with one of their worldly or local brews—the glassware alone makes for a superlative experience.

Weekend brunch is farm-fresh and just as popular.

◼ 837 W. Fulton Market (at Green St.)
🚇 Morgan
🖉 (312) 733-9555 — **WEB:** www.thepublicanrestaurant.com
◼ Lunch Sat – Sun   Dinner nightly   **PRICE:** $$

ORIOLE ✿✿
Contemporary

XxX | ✿ ♿ 🍴

Welcome to one of Chicago's greatest restaurants. The interior is mod yet industrial, with an open kitchen—filled with jovial professionals who look like they're cooking for a dinner party—that takes up a good deal of the space. The fact that nothing feels stuffy should not surprise since Oriole is something of a family business. Crisp attention to detail is clear in every member of this team, who are all thoroughly versed in the intricacies of the rather complex menu.

Laying aside his previous gluten-free cooking at Senza, Chef Noah Sandoval embraces all ingredients with contemporary edge and global flavors. Expect binchotan grilling, fresh pasta, frozen foam, and recurring flourishes like gastriques or Spanish cheeses.

The kitchen's opening salvo may feature a warm Scottish langoustine with white asparagus, a dollop of Kristal caviar, and torched lardo. This may be followed by jamón Ibérico de Bellota, served as a sort of "salad" with black walnut, bits of Campo de Montalban, and a drizzle of black pepper gastrique. Superb desserts courtesy of Pastry Chef/partner Genie Kwon pay homage to NOLA, like chicory custard with frozen whiskey foam, orange zest, and cinnamon-dusted vanilla ice cream.

■ 661 W. Walnut St. (at Union Ave.)
🚇 Clinton (Green/Pink)
℘ (312) 877-5339 — **WEB:** www.oriolechicago.com
■ Dinner Tue – Sat   **PRICE:** $$$$

ROISTER ✿
Contemporary

XX | 🍸 🍽

MAP: A1

Unapologetically loud, laid-back, and lively, Roister is the instant success from the Alinea Group. Even the ambient design reminds one of its sibling restaurants, though the cooking here, courtesy of Chef Andrew Brochu, is far more rustic.

The kitchen is boldly incorporated into the dining room and serves as its main focal point, adding to the synergy between front and back of house. Even service is a collaboration. The best seats are along the counter, before the kitchen's blazing hearth.

As expected, the food is creative and modern, but it is also soulful in incorporating its wood-fired hearth (don't miss the lasagna). Items may be served as small plates, family-style, or a tasting menu, culled from the à la carte offerings. Start with snacks like crisp-fried Yukon potato wedges dusted with soy and presented in a bowl with creamy tofu purée and rice vinegar. Mains include a whole chicken served as sweet tea-brined breast and crisp-skinned dark meat marinated in buttermilk and chamomile with creamy gravy and sunchoke hot sauce. For dessert, the poached apricot with sour cherry sorbet, fried almond crumble, and almond ice may sound straightforward, but is in fact beguilingly complex.

🔲 951 W. Fulton Market (bet. Morgan & Sangamon Sts.)
🚇 Morgan
📞 N/A — **WEB:** www.roisterrestaurant.com
🔲 Lunch & dinner daily

PRICE: $$$

SEPIA ✿
American

XX | 🕸 🍷 ♿ 🍴 🛁

When a restaurant's excellence is this consistent, it should come as no surprise that Michelle Obama named it one of her favorites. Set inside a 19th-century print shop, the historic dining room does a fine job mixing original details with modern touches. Muted tones in the exposed brick walls and custom tile floors complement newer elements like floor-to-ceiling wine storage and dramatic smoke-shaded chandeliers that drip with crystals.

Though the décor may tip its hat to yesteryear, Chef Andrew Zimmerman's cuisine is firmly grounded in the 21st century.

Meals here deliciously reflect the amalgam of American cuisine, with hints of Southeast Asian, Korean, and Mediterranean tastes. But, it is at dinner when this kitchen truly comes to life. Gnocchi may seem commonplace, but this version is memorable thanks to the flawless components and rich flavors of lamb sugo with ciabatta breadcrumbs. Chicken here is downright exciting, served crisp-skinned with a supremely buttery Albufera sauce, crumbly chestnuts, caramelized fennel, and sausage. Simple-sounding desserts keep the bar high until the very end, by way of offerings like toffee-coconut cake with chocolate ganache and burnt caramel.

▨ 123 N. Jefferson (bet. Randolph St. & Washington Blvd.)
🚇 Clinton (Green/Pink)
℘ (312) 441-1920 — **WEB:** www.sepiachicago.com
▨ Lunch Mon – Fri Dinner nightly   **PRICE: $$$**

SMYTH ❀ ❀
Contemporary

XxX | ♿ ⬚ 🍽️

Housed in what looks like an unremarkable industrial building, find a setting worthy of design magazine covers. Once inside, head upstairs to arrive at Smyth (Loyalist is a separate venue downstairs) and into its appealingly spare dining room, which feels so comfortable that it's easy to forget you're in a restaurant.

The service staff is hospitable, down to earth, and manages to keep the ambience relaxed despite the intensity of Chefs John Shields and Karen Urie Shields' extraordinary work. Beyond, their open kitchen mixes white tiles and cutting-edge equipment with a roaring hearth fire. There is a "come as you are" feeling among the crowd here, but everyone has dressed up a bit, as if in deference to the superb meal that awaits.

The cooking is unconventional and innovative, but by no means is it experimental. Instead, it delivers constant satisfaction alongside a few wow-inducing surprises. Unique combinations include the squab breast roasted with "fat back" for crackling skin that bursts with flavor, accompanied by crisped duck tongues and a scattering of black walnuts. Creativity may reach its height at dessert, in the salted licorice-cured yolk nestled in the smoothest fro-yo ever.

▉ 177 N. Ada St. (bet. Lake & Randolph Sts.)
▉ Ashland (Green/Pink)
📞 (773) 913-3773 — **WEB:** www.smythandtheloyalist.com
▉ Dinner Tue – Sat   **PRICE: $$$$**

SUSHI DOKKU 🐕

Japanese

🍴 | 🍶 ♿ 🏮 🧼   **MAP:** B2

Creatively adorned nigiri is the featured attraction at this hip sushi-ya that's all wood planks, stainless steel, chunky tables, and hefty benches.

Just one piece of Sushi Dokku's supple cuts showcasing quality and technique is not enough—thankfully each nigiri order is served as pairs. Among the terrific selection, enjoy the likes of hamachi sporting a spicy mix of shredded Napa cabbage, daikon, and red chili; or salmon dressed with a sweet ginger-soy sauce and fried ginger chips. South Pacific sea bream is deliciously embellished with a drizzle of smoky tomato and black sea salt. Those who wish to branch out from sushi should go for takoyaki (crispy fried octopus croquettes), grilled hamachi collar, or a brownie-crusted green tea-cheesecake.

- 823 W. Randolph St. (at Green St.)
- Morgan
- 📞 (312) 455-8238 — **WEB:** www.sushidokku.com
- Lunch Tue & Fri   Dinner Tue – Sat   **PRICE: $$**

SWIFT & SONS 🍴

Steakhouse

🍴🍴🍴 | 🎊 ♿ 🖥 🧼   **MAP:** A1

With the inception of this massive steakhouse at 1K Fulton, NY-based design firm AvroKO adds to their local portfolio in collaboration with Boka Restaurant Group. A renovated meat and produce warehouse built in the 1920s, the space unwinds from a raw bar aptly named Cold Storage into a plush hangout. Here, wood-trimmed archways and concrete columns modulate the scale of the rooms. The kitchen's contemporary take on steak serves up USDA Prime beef seared at high heat and presented with a trio of sauces. It's the kind of place where gluttony is rewarded (even their wine program features Coravin selections in three- or six-ounce pours. Extras like King crab Oscar and dessert (Boston cream pie?) are worth the calories.

Lunch is offered on weekdays at Cold Storage.

- 1000 W. Fulton Market (at Morgan St.)
- Morgan
- 📞 (312) 733-9420 — **WEB:** www.swiftandsonschicago.com
- Dinner nightly   **PRICE: $$$$**

NOTES

NOTES

MICHELIN
IS CONTINUALLY
INNOVATING
FOR SAFER, CLEANER,
MORE ECONOMICAL,
MORE CONNECTED
AND BETTER ALL
AROUND MOBILITY.

Tires wear more quickly on short urban journeys.

TRUE!

You tend to accelerate and brake more often when driving around town so your tires work harder!
If you are stuck in traffic, keep calm and drive slowly.

Tire pressure only affects your car's safety.

FALSE!

Driving with underinflated tires (0.5 below recommended pressure) doesn't just impact handling and fuel consumption, it will take 8,000 km off tire lifespan.
Make sure you check tire pressure about once a month and before you go on vacation or a long journey.

If you only encounter **winter weather from time to time** - sudden showers, snowfall or black ice - **one type of tire** will do the job.

?

TRUE!

The revolutionary **MICHELIN CrossClimate** - the very first summer tire with winter certification - is a practical solution to keep you on the road whatever the weather.

Fitting **2 winter tires** on my car guarantees maximum safety.

?

FALSE!

In the winter, especially when temperatures drop below 44.5°F, to ensure better road grip, all four tires should be identical and fitted at the same time.

2 WINTER TIRES ONLY =
risk of compromised road grip.

4 WINTER TIRES =
safer handling when cornering, driving downhill and braking.

If you regularly encounter rain, snow or black ice, choose a **MICHELIN Alpin tire**. This range offers you sharp handling plus a comfortable ride to safely face the challenge of winter driving.

MICHELIN

MICHELIN
IS COMMITTED

▶ MICHELIN IS THE **GLOBAL LEADER IN FUEL-EFFICIENT TIRES** FOR LIGHT VEHICLES.

▶ **EDUCATING YOUNGSTERS ON ROAD SAFETY FOR BIKES,** NOT FORGETTING TWO-WHEELERS. LOCAL ROAD SAFETY CAMPAIGNS WERE RUN IN **16 COUNTRIES** IN 2015.

QUIZ

1 TIRES ARE BLACK SO WHY IS THE MICHELIN MAN WHITE?

Back in 1898 when the Michelin Man was first created from a stack of tires, they were made of natural rubber, cotton and sulphur and were therefore light-colored. The composition of tires did not change until after the First World War when carbon black was introduced. But the Michelin Man kept his color!

2 HOW LONG HAS MICHELIN BEEN GUIDING TRAVELERS?

Since 1900. When the MICHELIN guide was published at the turn of the century, it was claimed that it would last for a hundred years. It's still around today and remains a reference with new editions and online restaurant listings in a number of countries.

3 WHEN WAS THE "BIB GOURMAND" INTRODUCED IN THE MICHELIN GUIDE?

The symbol was created in 1997 but as early as 1954 the MICHELIN guide was recommending "exceptional good food at moderate prices." Today, it features on the MICHELIN Restaurants website and app.

If you want to enjoy a fun day out and find out more about Michelin, why not visit the l'Aventure Michelin museum and shop in Clermont-Ferrand, France:

www.laventuremichelin.com

MICHELIN
A better way forward

INDEXES

ALPHABETICAL LIST OF RESTAURANTS

A

B

L

M

N

RESTAURANTS BY CUISINE

AMERICAN

ASIAN

AUSTRIAN

BARBECUE

BELGIAN

CHINESE

CONTEMPORARY

SPANISH

STEAKHOUSE

THAI

VEGETARIAN

VIETNAMESE

CUISINES BY NEIGHBORHOOD

ANDERSONVILLE, EDGEWATER & UPTOWN

American
ampersand wine bar ⃝ 18
gather ⃝ 21

Belgian
Vincent ⃝ 31

Contemporary
Elizabeth ❀ 22
Goosefoot ❀ 24

Ethiopian
Demera ⃝ 21
Ras Dashen ⃝ 29

French
Bistro Campagne ⃝ 20

Gastropub
Band of Bohemia ❀ 19
Hopleaf ⃝ 25

Indian
Mango Pickle ⃝ 27
Sabri Nihari ⃝ 29

Korean
Gogi ⃝ 23
Jin Ju ⃝ 25
San Soo Gab San ⃝ 30

Peruvian
Taste of Peru ⃝ 30

Seafood
Angry Crab (The) ⃝ 18

Southern
Big Jones ⃝ 20
Luella's Southern Kitchen ⃝ 26
Pearl's Southern Comfort ⃝ 27

Thai

Herb 🍴	23
Jin Thai 🍴	26

Vietnamese

Pho 777 🍴	28
Pho Xe Tang - Tank Noodle 🍴	28

BUCKTOWN & WICKER PARK ──────

American

Bristol (The) 🍴	40
Dove's Luncheonette 🍴	42
Trench 🍴	50
TWO 🍴	51

Barbecue

Lillie's Q 🍴	45

Contemporary

Ada St. 🍴	38
Mindy's Hot Chocolate 🍴	46
Schwa ❁	49

French

Le Bouchon 🍴	44

Fusion

Mott St. 🍴	47

Gastropub

Bangers & Lace 🍴	39
Dawson (The) 🍴	41
Owen & Engine 🍴	47

Indian

Cumin 🍴	41

International

Taus Authentic 🍴	48

Italian

Piccolo Sogno 🍴	48
tocco 🍴	50

Japanese

Arami 🍴	38
Izakaya Mita 🍴	44

Korean

En Hakkore 🍴	43

Mexican
Big Star ⬥○   39
Mexique ⬥○   46

Pizza
Coalfire Pizza ⬥○   40

Southern
Dixie ⬥○   42

Vegetarian
Green Zebra ⊛   43
Mana Food Bar ⊛   45

CHINATOWN & SOUTH

American
Promontory (The) ⬥○   61

Chinese
MingHin ⊛   60
Phoenix ⬥○   61

Contemporary
Acadia ❀❀   58

Deli
Eleven City Diner ⬥○   60

Indian
Chicago Curry House ⬥○   59

Italian
A10 ⬥○   59

GOLD COAST

American
Blue Door Kitchen & Garden ⬥○   69
Hugo's Frog Bar & Fish House ⬥○   70
NoMI Kitchen ⬥○   73

French
Bistronomic ⬥○   68
Bistrot Zinc ⬥○   68
Margeaux Brasserie ⬥○   71

Italian
Cafe Spiaggia ⬥○   69
La Storia ⬥○   70
Merlo on Maple ⬥○   72
Nico Osteria ⬥○   72

LAKEVIEW & WRIGLEYVILLE _____

LINCOLN PARK & OLD TOWN _____

WEST LOOP

STARRED RESTAURANTS

BIB GOURMAND

T

U

W

UNDER $25

Tell us what you think about our products.

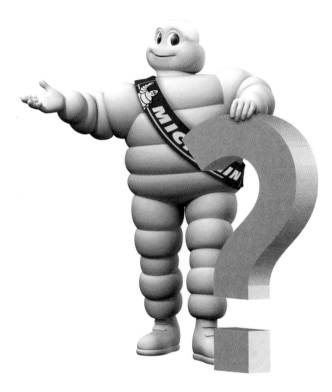

Give us your opinion

satisfaction.michelin.com

MICHELIN TRAVEL PARTNER

Société par actions simplifiées au capital de 11 288 880 EUR
27 Cours de l'Ile Seguin - 92100 Boulogne Billancourt (France)
R.C.S. Nanterre 433 677 721

© Michelin Travel Partner, All rights reserved
Dépôt légal septembre 2017
Printed in Canada - septembre 2017
Printed on paper from sustainably managed forests

Impression et Finition : Transcontinental (Canada)